30 DAYS to getting over the DORK you <u>used</u> to call your boyfriend

30 DAYS to getting OVER the DORK YOU USED to CALL YOUR boyFRiEND

A HEARTBREAK HANDBOOK
BY CLEA HANTMAN

DELACORTE PRESS

Published by Delacorte Press, an imprint of Random House Children's Books, a division of Random House, Inc., New York

www.randomhouse.com/teens

Educators and librarians, for a variety of teaching tools, visit us at www.randomhouse.com/teachers

Library of Congress Cataloging-in-Publication Data
Hantman, Clea.
30 days to getting over the dork you used to call your boyfriend / Clea Hantman. – 1st trade pbk. ed.
p. cm.
ISBN 978-0-385-73549-0 1. Single women—Psychology. 2. Man-woman relationships. 3. Separation (Psychology). 4. Self-help techniques. I. Title. II. Title: Thirty days to getting over the dork you used to call your boyfriend.
HQ800.2.H36 2008
155.6'423—dc22
2007005945

The text of this book is set in 13-point Mrs. Eaves.

Book design by Angela Carlino

Printed in the United States of America

10 9 8 7 6 5 4 3 2 1

First Edition

to all the dorks
i've loved before

30 DAYS to getting over the DORK you <u>used</u> to call your boyfriend

INTRODUCTION

Having trouble rising like a phoenix out of the dirty, stinky pile of ashes that was your last relationship? Can't get his voice, his face, his laugh out of your ever-lovin' mind? Feeling like a big lump of nothing since he dumped you?

Think you need a shoulder to cry on? Think again. What you need is a step-by-step program that will get you out of the doldrums, get him out of your life and refresh your sense of super-cute self so that you can go out there and conquer the world (and, more importantly, the foxy-boy population) once again.

Thirty days or less. That's all it takes.

Look, you've had a loss. It's bigger than losing your favorite sweater, smaller than the death of a favorite loved one, but it is a loss just the same. This thirty-day plan follows along to the tune of the five stages of grief—denial, anger, bargaining, depression and acceptance.

DENIAL. The "He'll be back" stage. The "I just need to call him and explain" stage. The innumerable drive-bys and/or stalking stage.

ANGER. Essentially, the "dickwad" phase. Voodoo dolls, revenge plotting, spreading heinous lies about him so that he is mortified beyond words—these are the things that haunt you.

BARGAINING. The truly ugly phase that is characterized by the unfortunate (and foul) "If only I were sweeter/prettier/sexier . . ." So wrong!

DEPRESSION. The classic "I'm going to die alone, never having had another boyfriend, and can you pass me that pint of triple mocha fudge" phase.

ACCEPTANCE. The zen "I think I'm gonna be all right" stage that we're striving for here. If we do our jobs right, it may even turn out to be the "I'm adorable, smart and cool!" phase.

Ultimately, it's all about your attitude. And you actually have all the power you need to change that, within you, right now. No matter how big the pain is, no matter how much it hurts, you have the power. By staying in this unhappy, miserable state, you are just hitting yourself in the face over and over. And frankly, you're waiting for someone else to pull you out of the funk. This book can help, but you're the one who has to do the pulling.

So here's the plan in a nutshell: we're going to shorten the healing process, limiting it to a month, tops, and along the way we're going to teach you a few things about yourself that I bet you didn't know (or at the very least forgot in the midst of this butt-ugly breakup). You'll also learn what to look for in your next conquests so that you can keep any future grand heartaches to a minimum.

The exercises in this book are designed to take you from lump on a log to bright and better than ever. With each task you'll find an inspirational haiku that will inform you of that day's mission. Perhaps they will motivate you to write your own healing haiku. And because music can be such an emotion instigator, each exercise is paired with a song. These tunes are there to help you reach deep down into your gut and find the meaning within—and then they'll inspire you to move on.

Keep this in mind as you work through the next

thirty days: change doesn't happen with a single, solitary action, like a boom! Change happens with a series of small actions. It takes a bit of time and some actual labor, but grand happenstances do not need to occur for this to work.

Your job is to listen, be patient, ask for help and make a genuine effort. It sounds sort of like school, but don't worry, this will be a whole lot more painful. Oh yeah, and fun too. Pinky swear.

DENIAL

The denial phase. It's characterized by the loud, anxious whine "It's not over, there is still hope," followed by a possessed call and/or e-mail attempting to convince the dork of this heinous hypothesis, topped off with the drive-bys that look for any glimpse of the dork, preferably in a state of heart-wrenching grief. Note: this is stalking. And it never ends well.

Before you begin, you need to start by accepting that the relationship is really over.

No more daydreaming about ways to get him back. No more anticipating the phone call that isn't coming. No more fantasizing about what brilliant thing you'll say to convince him that you are in fact the one.

Easy? No way. But once you get past this phase, you'll be positioned to move on with the rest of your life, which, in case you had any doubt, has yet to unfurl into its most awesome beauty. It's a cliché for a reason:

The best is yet to come.

In this chapter we are going to acknowledge the good as well as the bad, and then put a nice big "The End" exactly where it belongs: on the tail end, aka the butt, of this relationship.

Mantras for this chapter for you to repeat to yourself silently in times of need:
➤➤ I am so beyond this dork.
➤➤ There goes the dork, here comes my powerful self.
➤➤ Cuteness will come to me when I am ready.

DAY ONE: THE EXORCISM

How did this happen,
And where do we go from here?
Suck it up, baby.

You know how in an exorcism the priest needs to make sure the person is truly possessed first before proceeding? Well, same thing goes for you—you need to validate that this relationship existed before you can exorcise the aforesaid dork from your life. How do you do that? You write down your story.

Not his story. Not your best pals' version of what happened, or—crikey!—your mom's, but *your* story. Your story probably involves a lot of glossy, kissy loveliness, and that is A-okay, on this, the first day of getting over him. Allowing yourself to remember the pretty things is part of the process.

In a way, you're honoring the good stuff, honoring the part of you that put aside your scaredy-cat fears and became a part of someone else's life, no matter how long or how briefly. When your mind clears, you will see that you learned from this relationship, but that those lessons are not to be used on a new relationship with the dork. No, these are lessons that will benefit you and your future honeys.

So go ahead and grieve now. Crying is totally allowed over these next six days. Yikes, it's all but required. And here is the hokey but true part: once you've grieved over what is no more, you can step back and see what you have left, and you will see that it is in fact a whole lot.

ACTIVITY 1

This isn't the time to be self-conscious. Nobody has to know you did this—it's a private thing. Now, nab a pen, grab some paper and sit down alone. You can be in bed in your pajamas with a pint of something gooey by your side, you can be in a park under a tree with a warm breeze hitting your face, it doesn't matter. The key here is being alone and with a pen and paper.

Now start at the beginning: how did you meet, how did you first interact, what were the first words spoken? This is rough territory—gut-bustingly depressing—but today is the big day to wallow, so take full advantage and traipse through it all: the first kiss, the longing looks, the secret stuff.

Write on through to the other side—the end. Don't skip the middle, although if you're gonna skimp on any part, that's the one. Now write about the end: how it went down, the ugly words, the unspoken stuff.

When you're done, read it. If you must, read it again.

⦿ **VERY IMPORTANT** You must not show this story to the dork, and certainly not to anyone who could tell the dork, or much, much worse, show the dork. Instead, we will declare this story over and mark it with a ritual.

You'll need scissors. Personally I'm a fan of the kind with animal-shaped handles, but any will suffice. And really, you should be in your bedroom for this step. Now take the pages (or the novel, as the case may be) and stack them one on top of the other. Begin by cutting a long, thin strip of paper from the bottom to the top, along the right side. Continue cutting, moving left till you have no more sheets of paper, only strips.

Now stack the strips and cut them into small squares like . . . confetti.

Take the stuff by the handful, hold it close to your chest and with a rebel yell, let it fly up in the air.

I know; you're thinking, "Confetti? Party? This is so not a party." It's hard to see the healing process right now as related to a party in any way, but there will come a time in your life (quite possibly in the next twenty-nine days or so) when you will look back on this time and realize, yeah, it was something to celebrate and now it's time to celebrate its end.

Now vacuum the confetti all up and say, "*Adios, amigo,* you're hereby sucked up into a dark pit of nothingness."

SONG OF THE DAY:
NO DOUBT, "EX-GIRLFRIEND"

A seething song perfectly poised from the girl's perspective about how hard it can be to know that you kinda, sorta, deep down always knew it wouldn't end well. Play loud.

DAY TWO: PERFECT? HARDLY

It wasn't pretty.
Sometimes he smelled really bad,
But at times it rocked.

Sometimes when we look back on things that happened last year, or last month, or last week, or even yesterday, we have a tendency to rewrite history, retelling it with a rosy glow that wasn't present at the time. We make the bad junk seem teeny tiny and totally surmountable and the good stuff (and there was good stuff, there is no denying it) plentiful and overwhelmingly overwhelming.

But it wasn't exactly that way, was it?

We do this for a bunch of different reasons: We like wallowing in pain—it makes us feel connected to the ex. Or we just like the way wallowing makes us feel—important and real. Or it could be an almost automatic and innate thing, like how mothers forget the pain of childbirth because if they didn't, they would never ever have another baby. And in a way, relationships are like that too. We have to remember some good so we keep on keeping on, pursuing new (and better) relationships in the future. But to move on to greener pastures, we also have to acknowledge the bad so we can come to grips with why this one sucked and how the next one will be better. If we can't acknowledge what really happened, we can't learn from the experience. And if we can't learn from the experience, we are doomed to repeat it.

HARD-TO-SWALLOW RULE:
The relationship is over because something wasn't right.

And today we will blame the dork.

Yet another sheet or three of paper and a pen are needed. This time your friends can be involved, or not, although they will most certainly help add fuel to the fire. And that could be a good thing.

You're going to make a list of all the things that were wrong with the dork. Did he smell? Did he say he'd call and then not call? Did he have wholly unfortunate choices in footwear? Did he listen to really bad music? (Totally inexcusable in my book, but hey, that's just me.) They can be trivial. They can be huge. They should be trivial. They should be huge.

Ask your friends to contribute. I guarantee they will see things you totally did not. Don't be mad at them for it. Don't hold these things against them. They are helping you, assisting you the way they would a blind person who, though adept at getting around with a cane and a dog, occasionally needs help with directions.

❗ WARNING! And this is very important. Once again, you must not show this list to the dork, and certainly not to anyone who would or could tell the dork what's on it.

Next, study your list for a while. Don't be shy— you can even tape it to your closet door for a few hours. Just don't leave it there too long.

When you've seen enough of it, fold it up into a small square and tuck it into the toes of a pair of shoes you hardly ever wear. And there it shall stay. And when, one day, you decide to wear these shoes again, you'll find this list. And enough time will have passed that you can look at it again, only this time you'll be happy, because I almost guarantee you'll have an "Aha!" moment, one of those surprising and utterly lovely realizations that you were right, the dork was wrong and life goes on and on and on.

DAY THREE: THE DORK BOX

Burn, ignite, destroy,
Or leave strewn about your world?
Please! Box it, ship it!

It's pretty much a cliché to burn or destroy in some fashion (or at the very least toss out) everything the ex ever gave you. I don't subscribe to that practice. Don't get me wrong, it's not like I think you should keep all this crud around you, on your nightstand, in your locker or crowding the insides of your cute purse. But I don't think you should throw it in the gutter either.

There was an episode of *The Gilmore Girls* where Rory wanted everything from her ex, Dean, destroyed and out of the house. But her mom, Lorelei, knew better, so she packed it all up in a box and moved it to the back of her own closet. Not because she thought Rory and Dean were getting back together, but because she knew that these things marked a time in Rory's life that at the moment she wanted to forget. And while it was healthy for these objects to be out of sight, in the future she would not only be able to but might even *want* to look back on this stuff.

The interesting thing is, we sometimes hold on to these things, looking to them and even at them for clues and answers to the ever-present question— Why? But these things don't hold any answers or special meaning or insight. They are just that— things.

Still, later on, when our head has cleared and we have some distance from the situation, these very same things can be memory triggers of goodness. They can remind you not just of the dork, but of the times surrounding the dork . . . which is to say, they could remind you of yourself when you were feeling powerful and indestructible or when your friends were being extra-special awesome or some other fabulous nugget of time in the past when things were great. Think of it as sort of first-love paraphernalia, the stuff that allows you to remember what it was like when you were younger.

And that is why keeping some of the things that remind you of the dork, predork, is okay. But they need to be boxed up and shipped out. If you toss or ignite everything, you will regret it someday in the future.

Or maybe not, but let's just cover our bases.

ACTIVITY 3

This one is simple. Get a box. Fill it with a few items that remind you of the dork. Things given to you, things written to you, things the dork touched that just make you see his face every time you look at them.

Seal it, label it ("dork" will suffice) and hand it on over to a trusted friend or relative. Ask them to hide it. Ask them not to tell you where it is for at least two months. No matter what.

🔋 This is also the day we delete the dork from our cell phone memories, from our old-school phone books, from our e-mail address book and our IM list. It's time.

SONG OF THE DAY:
WILCO, "BOX FULL OF LETTERS"
A poetic song about the stuff one ex has left behind and how that stuff doesn't really help resolve any of the questions that abound around you.

19

DAY FOUR: SPEW YOU!

Toss that pain away.
Heave it, belch it, blow it out.
You feel better now?

If left to your own devices, you may just go on and on and on about the dork until you pass the point of receiving pity from others and move on to boring them, or worse, annoying them. And yet talking about it can be a good thing, like drop-kicking those noxious feelings straight out of your body. It can be good to review the turn of events and have friends point out the errors of the dork's ways. But on and on and on? Not so cool.

You know this already, I'm quite sure, but I'm just gonna remind you again since you're in a frag-ile, hazy-dazy state: **boys will come and boys will**

go, but your gal pals will stick with you through thick and thin.

This is the time to call upon their otherworldly powers of distilling the truth from the BS and delivering the finest-quality uplifting support. It is now, in your time of need, that they transform into shoulders to cry on and crutches to lean on. They're your superfriends, and they don't need bright spandex costumes to illustrate their awesome powers.

ACTIVITY 4

Gather as many of your friends together as you can for one giant spew session. Center stage is yours. Ask your friends to be the interactive audience for you this one last time. You are going to blow!

Set the date, set the time, pick a venue (your bedroom, a good friend's or even a coffee shop will work). If the spew session is going to happen at your house or someone else's, it would be a good idea to provide snacks. Snacks always make people more relaxed. Decorations are not necessary for such a shindig, but comfortable seating is key—pillows and soft couches or fluffy beds work wonders.

MY SPEW SESSION
(Record the details of your big blowout.)

Date:_____

Time: _____

Place: _____

Topic: _____
(fill in dork's name here)

Invitees: _____
_____
_____

Style: (circle one)
➤ Slumber-Party Chic
➤ Parisian Coffeehouse
➤ New Orleans Voodoo Parlor
➤ Soap-Opera Opulence
➤ Other _____

Menu: (aka Snacks to Be Served) _____
_____
_____

Sound Track:_____
_____
_____
_____
_____

Once everyone is there, it's your time to cry, scream, rant, rave, bitch, moan, gripe, swear, curse and all-around unload. Your friends' jobs are to be present, positive, and attentive; to chime in if need be; to sympathize profusely and to all-around uplift you.

This session should go on for a preset amount of time—a couple of hours if everyone's available; otherwise, an hour or so will have to do. And then, when it's all done, it's done. Of course, your feelings aren't done and gone. Hardly. But the spewing? The rehashing at length of what went wrong and what could I have done differently and what's wrong with me?

That's over, Rover.

It's not that you can't ever mention the dork's name again, but it's time, here at Day Four, to relinquish some of that divine right to invoke his name in a whiny tone at every turn, whenever the mood strikes. It's time to try a little bit harder, to exert a bit more effort to not talk about him morning, noon and night. Yes, it's work, but no one ever said this could all be executed from a horizontal position on the couch.

SONG OF THE DAY:
SIA, "BREATHE ME"

A haunting, shiver-inducing song of sadness with a touch of light in the center, thanks to the friendship that helps breathe life back into her cold body. Listen, cry if you must, and then move on.

DAY FIVE: BAD HABITS

Before, I felt whole.
Now only a half remains.
"Hogwash!" cries the crowd.

So perhaps it's the long walk to class, now spent alone, that has your heart in a vise, because the dork used to walk with you. Or maybe it's not the walk to class but the call that used to take place every night at seven p.m. Or Saturday evenings, when you were always together and now you're not. What I'm saying is, sometimes our old routines are harder to let go of than our actual feelings for the dork.

Often, we like the idea of the boyfriend (and the idea that you're half of this super-cool exclusive thing: a couple) and the perks of the boyfriend (someone who's there for you always, at least in theory) almost as much as we like the actual guy. Sometimes we like these things *more than* the actual guy. Bottom line, these things are miss-able, and you can grieve over them too. But then it's time to shake up the old routines and make new ones so that these minuses from your life aren't staring you in the face daily. And who knows, you may even find a few new pluses.

It can be a daunting task, but it's not really that hard to do. Sometimes all you need is a pal to walk those same halls with you so you're no longer alone. And sometimes it may be to take a new route altogether.

ACTIVITY 5

On the next page, we have two columns. On the left side, write down some of those so-called routines that involved you and the dork. You know what I mean—things you did religiously, regularly. A date, a place you went, a time of day you spoke to or saw each other.

In the right-hand column, come up with some sort of alternative to the activity on the left: write down "get new companion," or think of another activity to take your mind off that particular routine. It can be as simple as taking a bath instead of thinking about the phone call that's not gonna happen. Taking a bath is something you probably haven't done since you were a kid and is lovely and relaxing and cleansing (literally and figuratively) and preferably done while reading a gossip magazine. Or it could be reading a book in bed, hanging with friends, playing a board game with your sister or brother, calling a good friend on the phone to talk about the latest celebrity gossip (but not the dork), having a cup of coffee with a pal, going for a run, walking a different way to class, whatever. You're simply replacing an old habit with a shiny brand-new one.

ROUTINE	ALTERNATIVE

Now here comes the slightly harder part: you must execute the actions on the right side of the page. From here on out, they are part of your new routine. And no looking back.

SONG OF THE DAY:
*NSYNC, "BYE BYE BYE"

That's right, it's time for some serious Cheez Whiz. It doesn't get cornier than this, so play it loud and play it proud, and you better sing along.

DAY SIX: FRIENDSHIP ROCKS

Boys will come and go,
But so does the mailman, right?
Your girl squad kicks butt.

Sometimes when we're in a relationship we neglect our day-in-and-day-out pals. It's not hard to see why—it's pretty much basic math: you have less free time, the free time you probably dedicated to those friends predork. Well, the god of math is shining brightly on you and your friends today, because you've miraculously regained your time. Call them.

Pretty much any self-help book, any book about grieving over loss or death, is going to start by directing you to your friends. And it makes sense: they know you. They probably knew you even predork. They see what you've lost and what you've gained.

They care about your well-being, your happiness and your pain.

It's time to acknowledge your pals, not spew at them about your life's tragic turns (we did that a few days ago, remember?).

Today is about you and them, not him.

ACTIVITY 6

In the book and the movie *The Sisterhood of the Traveling Pants*, the girls have this little ceremony to honor their friendship. It involves candle lighting, sitting in a circle and making proclamations. You see where I'm going with this?

You can invite an entire posse of girlfriends or choose just one or two (and if you do only choose one, choose the person who makes you feel the best inside—the one who lifts you up when you're down).

Make it extra-special by bringing in candles or mood lighting; make sure you have comfy surroundings and great music in the background. And then start asking questions: "What's happening with you, friend?" (Okay, it sounds super-dorky when you ask it like that, so go ahead and use your pal's name in that sentence instead.) Ask her how things are at home, at school, at her clubs or any teams she's on. You can even ask her about her romantic life. I know this one will be harder than the rest, but remember that if hers is sweet and swell, then that's a good thing, and you can use your friend's experiences as inspiration for your own future endeavors. If her romantic life is on a downward spiral, listen and be there. But try hard, call on all your inner strength, to not just start bitching about your own agony. It's not about him. It's about you and your pal.

You can do the candle-sitting-in-a-circle-making friendship-proclamations thing. Or you can come up with another exciting and personal way to celebrate the rebonding of your friendship.

Other good things to do with your pal(s) to reclaim your friendship:
➤➤ Find a photo booth and take a whole lotta strips of photos
➤➤ Make a scrapbook together of the silliest parts of your friendship, one that includes the worst pictures and goofiest pictures and the laugh-out-loud pictures, or make a big bulletin board that can go from one friend's house to the other's each week
➤➤ Take a jewelry-designing class together at the local bead shop
➤➤ Make a special lunch date for every Saturday afternoon
➤➤ Cook up a yummy dinner together
➤➤ Record a conversation about the silliest of things and make CDs for everyone on the recording
➤➤ Make up your own language and then speak only in that tongue all day

CHAPTER ONE IS OVER.

Does that mean that the denial is over?

Not exactly. But it is controlled—or at least managed. It has been addressed.

Accepting that you're in a blah mood and not feeling so hot right now doesn't mean you *enjoy* feeling like this. Or that you want to continue feeling like this. It just means we are all acknowledging it. We are not denying it. And if you deny it, if you ignore it or you stay tuned in to your iPod 24-7 without thinking about what has happened, you run the risk of getting trapped inside this blechy, craptastic mood for longer than necessary.

So swirl the bad taste in your mouth around a bit. Know it, feel it.

And rejoice in your completion of the first six days of the road trip to removing the dork from your life. You've already replaced bad habits with good ones and acknowledged your pals. You done good.

Now call on that inner bitch, because it's time to move on. It's time to get angry.

31

ANGER

So you've had a few days of lovey-dovey fun and kindness, some quality friend time, and that was rocking, but it's not like that anger you had just seeped out the pores of your body never to return again.

Oh no, the anger still lives in your shoulders, your temples, your hips. Heck, even in your knee-caps and your big toe. In fact, it may be worse than at the very beginning. Sometimes it takes a week for the genuine resentment to kick in and kick back.

Why do we feel angry? It may be obvious, or it may be hard to put your finger on, but I think at the heart of it, the reason for your anger can be as primal as a completely ugly disfigured desire to get back at someone. And when you put it that way, it doesn't sound so rewarding. And that's the thing—most of the time (not all the time, but seriously, most of the time), we don't feel better after we've gotten revenge or gotten a person back. In fact, what we usually feel is crappy about ourselves, like how did we go that far? How could we have? In other words, we end up feeling ugly inside.

And when we do spew anger or get back at someone or embark on a crazy plot of revenge, we're just making the anger and bitterness bigger. Like we're involving other people now and they're getting sucked into the vortex that is a deep, oozing black hole of resentment and anguish. We're spreading it around like flyers for a concert, only this isn't a concert, this is your anger. And there aren't any Twizzlers at your anger party.

But here is the ironic part: if we don't acknowledge that we're pissed off and want revenge, if we don't talk about our anger or write about it (not act on it), then we're really just sitting on it, holding it down till it regains its strength and takes over our bodies forevermore. For the next few days you want to feel the anger, walk with it by your side, explore it but never direct it at anyone. If we work this angry stuff out now, we'll be less likely to spread it around.

And so that brings us to this: choice. You actually can make the choice to keep your anger in and live with it day in and day out (no fun), or you can make the choice to walk through these next six days with "Effort" as your middle name. Then you can choose to say "Fare thee well, anger, I hardly knew you," and you can really and truly let it go. Choice. It totally looks good on you.

DAY SEVEN: ANGER MANAGEMENT

Night falls grimly now.
My thoughts are wild beasts of rage.
Counting calms me down.

You know what I think is the hardest part of the day during this unfortunate time of suffering?

No, not seeing the dork.

It's the time right before I fall asleep—or rather, before I *try* to fall asleep. Lying there in bed, all I can think about is everything. I run through conversations we had, fights we didn't. Imagine scenarios where I may see said dork, words I would say and many more I wouldn't. I try to read the dork's mind at that very moment, conjure up places the dork has been and who he's been with. I sweat with anger and rage and my exhausted body turns restless and fidgety. I dream up solutions that are crazed and inappropriate because it's late at night and I'm not in my right mind.

But how can you avoid that quiet time? Turning the TV on only serves to make my thoughts louder in an effort to drown out another late-night rerun of *Saved by the Bell* (it's always on at three in the morning, and unfortunately, I know this firsthand). Movies just make me cry. Books have good intentions written all over them, but they rarely work.

The seething turns to resentment, which turns to agitation, which turns to wrath, which turns to another sleepless night. Finally, in the wee hours of the morning, my mind and body shut down, too weak from all the stress I've put them through to go on. And then when my alarm goes off, I wake up from my hour or so of bad sleep and I look like hell, which just brings all that anger right back front and center.

Sound familiar?

ACTIVITY 7

The trick is to take command of your mind before your body is horizontal.

As you ready yourself for bed by brushing your teeth and washing your face, start thinking of a relaxing place. For me, that's a place where the sun is shining and the waves are crashing. So for example's sake, let's run with that one. Think about an empty beach and think about the smells, the salt water, the sand, the warm breezes.

Keep thinking of this place as you lie down in bed. Get in a comfortable position and close your eyes. Now imagine you're lying on that beach, on the sand. Start at your toes and let your mind walk up your body from the bottom to the top, and as you go, release the tension from each segment of your body. All it takes is thinking about that one spot and it naturally goes limp. Try it. Think "relax arches," and they sort of fall just a little. The mind is powerful. Now work your way up your body. Relax your feet, ankles, calves, thighs, hips, lower back, shoulders, arms, hands, neck and most importantly and last, your jaw and temples.

Now imagine you're on a raft, one of those really expensive rafts that are more comfortable than any bed. And you're floating on the pristine crystal blue ocean. Feel the breeze, smell the salty air. Now count the waves as they pass under your body, under your raft, but count backward, from twenty. Slowly, as slowly as waves roll on the ocean. And breathe deeply along to the rhythm of the ocean. Twenty, nineteen, eighteen, and so on. If you get to one and you're not relaxed enough to sleep, count from twenty again. By focusing your mind so specifically on nature and numbers, you force your body to disengage and delve into a deep sleep.

Of course, the beach doesn't work for everyone. You may need to place yourself in a peaceful mountain cabin or even a gorgeous chamomile-scented spa.

Or maybe you need something completely different and much less holistic: put yourself in the middle of this (or any other nondork-related) wonderful dream where Jake Gyllenhaal and Orlando Bloom are fighting over you. Each is romancing you in an effort to win your heart, mind and body. Imagine the exotic locations, the conversation, the inevitable long and languid kiss. . . . you'll be sleeping peacefully in no time.

Take a moment to write about your "calm place" or a situation that makes you feel altogether peaceful and serene. What does it smell like? How does the air feel? Is it hot or cool? What do you feel beneath your feet? What can you touch? What can you see? If you run out of room, continue on your own notebook paper.

_____

_____

_____

_____

_____

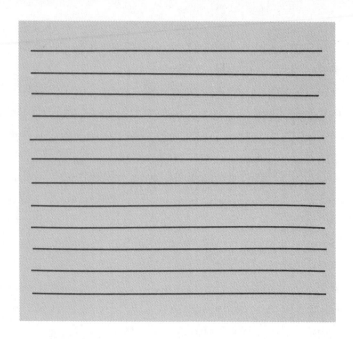

DAY EIGHT: WALK ON

Step and stomp and crash—
Makes me laugh and laugh and laugh,
Like crazy magic.

Let's get one thing straight today: you are not a victim. Yes, breaking up sucks, and some things may have been out of your control, but being a victim, in this case, is letting other people's ideas of you, or vision of you, be *your* vision of you.

They don't know *all of you*—only you do. This is starting to sound like a Dr. Seuss book, but my point is, don't judge yourself by the way other people see you. Judge yourself by the person you are inside and the person you project on the outside. View yourself as the whole person that you know you are.

Back to that victim thing: I want you to take control

of your life, your personality and your anger, and this bizarre little exercise just may go a long way to helping you do that, even though it is by far one of the simplest tasks in this here book. At the risk of sounding like some crackpot on the Self-Realization Channel, you have the power. And today you're going to use it.

Oh, and you know that old adage "laughter is the best medicine"? It's certainly the best cure for anger. Today I urge you to express a bit of anger, but to laugh a little too.

ACTIVITY 8

Write down the dork's name on a piece of masking tape. Then write down a whole sentence, something the dork did or said that makes your skin crawl. Write it boldly and beautifully on the tape with a big ol' Sharpie pen. Write another sentence. And another. And then stick the tape to the soles of your shoes. Put one or two pieces on the bottom of each shoe; don't show preferential treatment to the right or the left.

And then go about your day.

Periodically walk with a bit more pressure and power in your step. Maybe even jump up and down a few times. Grind your feet into the turf below you over and over again. You'll forget about it from time to time and then you'll remember, and when you do, do a little *Stomp*-inspired jig.

And in the end—well, did you laugh? Did you laugh about how fun it was to step all over the ex? Wasn't it silly how much pleasure you derived from this little experience, this little guilty pleasure that caused no one pain or harm or sadness? It was just between you and your shoes—and that's a very good thing.

SONG OF THE DAY:
YEAH YEAH YEAHS, "MAPS"
A great stomping song. Put your soul-baring soles on and pretend you're singer Karen O in your bedroom, leaping around and wailing to the backbreaking beat of your heart.

DAY NINE: FOCUS-POCUS

Everyone quiet!
My insides are still so loud.
Silence, oh silence.

When I get angry (and I do), my body gets this nervous Ping-Pong energy inside, like there are zillions of tiny red-hot BBs pulsating through my veins and bouncing off the inner walls of my skin. And then my outer layer of skin, the one the whole world sees, shakes and shivers and moves nervously about. And unfortunately they, my inner motion and outer motion, seem to be running at different speeds altogether, which only makes me feel dizzy and an all-around mess.

How does anger translate into a physical response for you? Does it make you sluggish and lethargic and clumsy? Or heavy and forceful and plodding? Or does it affect you like it does me, making you nervous and edgy and spun out?

No matter how your body reacts when it's angry, there's a way to calm it down. It's time to pull out your yin-yang charms, turbans and finger cymbals.

Just kidding! No turbans necessary. But seriously, turning to the New-Ageiness of all things Eastern and meditative is not a bad thing. Meditation—which in its most basic form is really just quieting the mind—is a miraculous way to handle the heebie-jeebies. And so is yoga, or exercise of any kind, but more on that later.

Today we concentrate on the act that is meditation. No, you don't have to sit in silence for eons. But you *can* pull from this short (promise) exercise when your body just seems out of your control. And that out-of-control feeling is something we are seriously looking to neutralize.

ACTIVITY 9

Sit on the floor or in a chair, it doesn't matter. What *does* matter is that your back and spine are straight and your head is high. You may feel stiff sitting like this, so take a second to relax your jaw and shoulders. Place your palms together and then bend your thumbs so the knuckles protrude. Take those thumb knuckles and lightly press them into your sternum, at the level of your heart (there is almost like a little notch the perfect size just waiting for knuckles—didn't know that, did you?) Keep them there. Now take a breath: slow, deep, smooth. Take it and imagine it traveling down your windpipe and into your belly. Now close your eyes and follow that breath, imagining its journey into your body, into your lungs and back out again. Focus on how it feels; draw a mental picture of what it looks like. This is called visualization. Once you're in the groove of it, think about the pressure you're putting on your sternum. Can you feel your heart beat? Listen, and visualize the heart beating. Do this for a few moments, taking in the pure magic of your functioning body.

Now release your hands and rub them together. Rub them until the palms are warm and toasty and almost electric with the energy of the friction, and then place your right palm on your chest, in the center, and the left palm on top of that. Close your eyes. Do you feel the warmth? The energy in your chest? Give that energy a color—your favorite color—and then visualize that colorful energy glowing in your chest and radiating into other parts of your body. Follow the color through your body; feel it; concentrate on that color and that energy. When you've had enough, let go of your chest and hold your hands out, slowly stretching your arms straight.

If you feel up to it, send that colorful energy out into the world, like you're some do-gooder hippie superhero. Imagine it flowing from all your limbs out into the air, where it will hitch a ride on some unsuspecting yet lucky person.

Before getting up, inhale and exhale slowly and carefully; then open your eyes gently. In other words, don't just jump up from this exercise with an "okay, cross that one off the list" attitude, but rather, ease out of the altered state you were (hopefully) in. And next time you're feeling aggro or nervous or full of rage, go off for a few minutes and feel the meditation love.

SONG OF THE DAY:
MODEST MOUSE, "FLOAT ON"

A song filled to the brim with the same "let it all go" attitude of a meditation session. Float on indeed. Listen after a round of quiet time with yourself.

DAY TEN: GET PHYSICAL

Downward dog goes ruff—
Oh! Then he pees on my leg.
Bad doggy, bad dog.

Do you play sports? Run? Exercise at all? If you do and you have been, I suspect your anger isn't as fierce as, say, your neighbor's is. You know—the one who watches a whole lot of bad TV.

There is scientific proof that exercise releases endorphins, which are like self-generating good-mood pills for your body. At the risk of sounding like your gym teacher, exercise makes you feel good in so many ways: You feel better about yourself physically and mentally. It releases the squeezing sensation from your muscles and forces them to relax. When you feel strong you can't help feeling good about yourself. When you

exercise during the day, you sleep more soundly at night. Plus, a good sweat cures many of life's ills.

But alas, many of us suck at the sports thing. It's something to do with a lack of coordination. Even something as simple and basic as running is difficult for me: my ankles knock together and I end up bruised, or worse—flat on my face.

So what's a girl to do if she suffers from this unfortunate sorry-at-sports affliction?

Yoga. It actually takes very little skill, only small droplets of coordination (and really, it's possible with no coordination; your yoga just won't be as pretty as your pal's). And it's bizarrely calming, something you may be in dire need of.

Now, if you are terrific at sports and hitting the field or gym or court on a regular basis, do not skip today's exercise—I repeat, do not skip today's exercise—because yoga is so good at stretching the body out, it can actually prepare it for other exercise. Plus, I've included a simple "yoga move" at the end that has nothing to do with sports and everything to do with Narnia. Intrigued? Read on anyway.

ACTIVITY 10

Time for yoga! Following is just a smattering of poses and exercises. For more information, go online, pick up a yoga mag or book or DVD at the library or

watch a yoga show on television. For now, read on, work out each pose slowly until you get it and then spend ten minutes (or more) running through the various poses, one after the other. And don't forget to breathe.

STANDING FORWARD BEND

One of the most basic yoga poses is also one of the best. Simply put, this is you, standing up straight, taking a deep breath and on the exhale bowing as far down as you can. Stretch to touch your toes and then send your arms back behind you and up in the air; then clasp your fingers together and pull up with your hands, stretching your back. Release and slowly come back up to a standing position.

DOWNWARD DOG

If you're familiar with yoga at all, you've surely heard of the downward dog. Lay down a towel—or a mat, if you have one—and get on all fours. Align your hands on the ground below your shoulders, your knees below your hips. Now inhale and curl your toes under, lift those hips and stretch the back of your thighs. Exhale and press down with your heels. As you push, feel the strength of your arms and legs and how it extends through your body and onto the ground. Breathe. Breathe again. And again. And now you're done.

TOE REACH and FISH POSE

Lie on your back and lift your legs to the sky. Breathe in and then lift your shoulder blades off the ground. As you exhale, reach your right hand toward your left foot (relax the other arm). It's important to stretch to reach—don't bounce. Inhale as you drop your legs, but keep your shoulders up, and then exhale as you take your left hand up toward your right foot. Repeat. After the toe reach, it's a great idea to go into the fish pose: lie flat on the ground and then sit up on your elbows, bringing your hands, palms down, under your butt. Now slowly arch your back, pressing your weight into your elbows and butt until your head just grazes the ground.

Breathe through your nose for thirty seconds and release. Repeat.

LOCUST POSE

Lie on your belly this time and clasp your hands behind your back. Inhale and stretch your body forward, lifting your chest off the ground but keeping the tops of your feet flat and still on the ground. Exhale and lift your arms up slightly higher. Hold and then release. Repeat.

THE ASLAN POSE

This is a yoga pose for the face. In some circles it's called the lion pose, but since I'm a fan of the Chronicles of Narnia, I prefer to call it the Aslan pose, after the noble lion warrior. If your head is aching from the mish-mash of bad feelings circling your brain, this will help. Promise. Sit or stand, but make sure your back is straight and your shoulders are relaxed. Now inhale and scrunch up your face tight, squeeze your eyes closed, raise your shoulders up to your ears, clench your fists, and pucker up the ol' kisser. Hold like that for a few seconds and then exhale and open your eyes wide, as wide as they can go, and your mouth too. Stick out your tongue. Spread your fingers till they ache a bit, release those shoulders and let out a monosyllable. You know, like "Ha!" or "Oy!" Repeat when necessary.

Now, if all this yoga stuff just isn't for you, well, do you have a hula hoop?

I kid you not, hula-hooping engages your mind (you have to concentrate), frees the hips and makes you laugh. So if all else fails, haul the hula hoop out of the garage and shake it like a Polaroid picture.

SONG OF THE DAY:
JUANA MOLINA, "LA VERDAD"
Mystical-sounding, with animal and jungle noises and elegant lyrics in Spanish. Listen during your yoga cooldown.

DAY ELEVEN: ROLE CALL

I can do it now.
I have learned so much from you.
Thank you, Madonna.

Who inspires you?

Who makes you feel like you can achieve anything?

Who do you believe in?

All too often the answer to these questions is "no one." But role models are important. And I don't mean role models as in people you want to dress like or look like. I mean role models who inspire you. Who excite you. Who make you feel and think and dream.

I'm talking about people who have done something with their lives, and by that I don't necessarily mean huge things, but things that changed their world and made it better. Your parents. A teacher. A favorite writer. A favorite musician. Inspiration can come from a small place or a big place; it can center on a minuscule idea or a humongous one.

ACTIVITY 11

Look around today. Look at the people you know; look at the last book you enjoyed or the hobbies you have. Maybe look at the careers of people who are doing what you think you might want to do in the future.

You're looking for people doing cool stuff. People who inspire you. People who rock.

And here's the potentially hard part of today's exercise: don't settle on actors or musicians or models just because they are cool. You're looking for something more. They may inspire an outfit, but today, look beyond the clothes.

For instance, I admire Zach Braff's chutzpah, creativity and smarts—he took his status as a sitcom star and made his own indie movie that was hilarious and touching and featured awesome bands on the sound track. I delight in the way the Hold Steady singer Craig Finn has visited high schools in an effort to demystify the whole "rock star" persona. I adore the elaborate literary quality of singer and pianist Regina Spektor's songs and am fascinated and inspired by her tough moves from Russia to Austria to Italy and finally to New York. And I even admire Angelina Jolie's global outlook and the way she has focused a lot of her attention—and therefore much of this country's attention—on places in need.

So now, come up with one, two, five role models—however many really and truly mean something to you. Don't give up if you can't find one just yet. If you explore the things you're really interested in and like, you're bound to come up with one, and a *good* one.

Now think about that person. What is it about her? Does she seem to have a crazy drive heretofore unknown in a human being? Is she outrageously kind and selfless? Is she witty and clever and that's how she comes up with the genius? And write these things down randomly. If this is someone you know or if it's someone someone you know knows, ask about her. Think about her characteristics and joys and practices and efforts. If it's someone you can look up online, do it. Research her to learn more about her. You're looking for the goods that make her who she is.

On the next page, write down the name of a person you admire. And if you run out of room, just grab a piece of paper. (And remember—it doesn't have to be a girl!)

I admire _____

because _____

_____

_____

_____

I admire her [or him] because _____

_____

_____

_____

_____

Oh wait, there is more: _____

_____

_____

_____

_____

Once you're done, look at what you've written. Are there things you have in common with this person? Are there things you can develop and work on that could create in you more qualities like this role model's? Write those down too.

If you're having trouble, here's a cheat sheet of qualities and attributes—just circle the ones you admire!

➤ adaptable
➤ artistic
➤ brilliant
➤ cautious
➤ clever
➤ confident
➤ creative
➤ dynamic
➤ energetic
➤ enthusiastic
➤ generous

➤ happy
➤ healthy
➤ hopeful
➤ humorous
➤ idealistic
➤ independent
➤ intelligent
➤ inventive
➤ kooky
➤ logical
➤ mature

➤ modest
➤ original
➤ persevering
➤ polite
➤ positive
➤ progressive
➤ realistic
➤ spontaneous
➤ spunky
➤ strong
➤ trustworthy

Now you have more than just a role model. You have a sense of how and why she's (or he's) your role model and how and why you are like her (or him). It's a page of inspiration. Treasure it.

SONG OF THE DAY:
MARIT LARSEN, "ONLY A FOOL"
A light little ditty about walking away from a dork and not looking back. This Norwegian pop chick has just the right amount of sass for Day Eleven. Dig the slide whistle.

DAY TWELVE: HOMEWORK

Spit, scream, yell, cuss, maim—
And use pretty penmanship.
Stash away for good.

This is not an earth-shattering idea. Most every self-help book in the world will tell you to allow your feelings to explode onto paper with a venomous rage. And they all also tell you to then hide that letter away. Either that or destroy it. But you never, ever send it.

Even if it seems a bit like we're taking a step backward, don't skip activity 12. The anger hasn't left the building altogether. We need these little releases throughout the "getting over it" process to stay on course. These moments propel us forward even as it seems that we are moving back. It's time to summon the classic angry woman scorned, only you're gonna make her less clichéd and way more personal.

Once again, grab some paper and a pen. A pen you really, really like to write with, one that doesn't hurt your hand even after plentiful paragraphs. Get cozy. And then tell the dork everything you've ever thought about telling him. All the good (if you can recall any of that) and definitely all the bad. Feel free to use cusswords if that's your thing. You can call him every name in the book. You can write in list form or letter form. You can wish horrible things to happen to him that in the "real world" would make you want to go to confession even if you were not a religious person. In other words, screw karma; no one has to know you're wishing these horrid things upon him. Just go for it. Only you and the paper know. And maybe your teddy bear. Do it till your hand hurts even though you're writing with that favorite pen. But do it in one sitting. No turning back to it when you're done. This letter has no "to be continued."

When you're finished, read through it once and feel the satisfaction of the explosion. Now let's turn that eruption into something positive.

We're going to make beads. I know, random! But not really.

You'll need **SCISSORS,** a **GLUE STICK** or some other kind of plain ol' glue, a **COUPLE OF WOODEN SKEWERS** (toothpicks will work in a pinch, or even a few straws will do) and last, **SOME CLEAR NAIL POLISH.**

➡➡ Cut your letter into long, slender triangles, the shape of a thin slice of pizza. At their widest (on the crust side) they should be as wide as you want your bead to be. Want a one-inch bead? Then cut the wide end of your triangle one inch across. Cut up the whole letter like this, even if it's two or three or eight pages long.

➡➡ Now put glue on the entire backside of the triangle, but stop about a half inch from the wide end. Place the skewer (or toothpick or straw) at the wide end and roll. The paper will wrap around and around the skewer, creating the bead (the hole is where the skewer is!). It's the triangular shape you cut that makes a cool tapered effect.

➡➡ Now apply some nail polish to the whole "bead." It acts like glue and gives it a nice glossy finish—plus, it ensures that no one can unroll the paper and see what it said, *including you.*

➡➡ Repeat. The skewer can hold a few beads at a time.

➤➤ Now balance your skewer(s) across the top of a cup or bowl to dry (that way the beads are suspended in the air for better all-over drying.)

➤➤ When they're dry, string the beads into a necklace, bracelet or key chain. You just turned something bad and ugly into something quite sweet and totally DIY. Not so random anymore. Congratulate yourself.

And feel good—there is only one more letter-writing homework assignment left in this book, and it doesn't come until the end.

SONG OF THE DAY:
BEN FOLDS FIVE, "SONG FOR THE DUMPED"
Fury, hilarious fury about a boy who has been dumped, complete with smarmy sarcasm. Play this one loud while you write, and don't forget to sing along at the top of your lungs.

CHAPTER TWO IS OVER.

And I'd bet two sweaters and a donkey that your anger has lessened dramatically since the start of this book. You're feeling at least a little calmer. The edge of madness has been filed down, and that's important because it allows you to levelheadedly move on and address the much bigger questions that lurk in your mind.

But first, take a moment to relish the tranquility (or something approximating it). The work you have done thus far is emotionally draining yet invigorating, no? Harnessing your very own mind-control power to make the hurt a bit more bearable, well, that's a mighty cool thing. That's something to be proud of right here, right now.

BARGAINING

Why did this happen to me?
  Why is bad stuff always happening to me?
  Nothing good ever happens to me.

Do you ever find yourself repeating those lines while rocking back and forth in a hazy stupor? Most of us have been there at some time or another.

Bad stuff happens to everyone. But so does good stuff. It's just that we remember the bad, achy-breaky stuff, especially when we're in a furiously futile fetal position. Right about then, the good stuff tends to go by the wayside all too easily.

It's time to stop feeling sorry for yourself. Stop

thinking that you're the only one in the world who has been rocked by a bad relationship. It happens.

If you stay in the mood you're in for too long, you run the risk of having more cruddy stuff happen before the good stuff can hit you. Because this mood you're in permeates everything you do. It gets into crevices and stays there like belly-button dirt. And not until you shake free of it (or give it a really good scrubbing) are you getting out from under the crap.

You need to learn how to welcome the good, invite it in, give it a place to get all cozy so it stays for a while.

You also need to figure out what you want, as well as what you *don't* want. It's kind of like being informed about political candidates—to make the best choices you need to know as much about the topics as you can.

The topics on the table this week? Love, values, good qualities and bad ones too. Let's learn about 'em together, shall we?

DAY THIRTEEN: PITY PARTY

Hear that sound? Moaning?
Oh wait, it comes from within.
I feel very sick.

Are you replaying the scenes of the breakup over and over in your head? Have you found yourself reenacting these scenes for people, still, even though I asked you politely not to?

You get a perverse sort of pleasure out of the retelling, don't you? I mean, there is some sort of sick and weird comfort we get by running through the breakup a thousand times. Don't be embarrassed; it happens to the best of us. It's called self-pity, and it's a wacky thing. It can take over our bodies and our minds and hang on our heavy limbs and drag us down to the ground. At first, it seems that this self-pity machine, the one that has you telling and retelling the same stories over and over, is helping you heal. But at some point, self-pity goes beyond helping and becomes far more than merely harmless, and eventually it can turn into the problem itself. When you're truly grieving, your pals will ache to help you. But when you're fishing for pity, your pals will ache to hurt you.

A very wise person once called self-pity "the replay button." You're just running through the same old, same old again, and you know what happens when you're busy running through the old over and over? You miss out on what's happening right now. You miss out on new stuff happening around you. You plain miss out.

I'm gonna ask you to move on and stop replaying and retelling and reagonizing. But this time I would like you to listen to me. Yeah, it takes work. In fact, it takes more work than just stopping yourself every time you feel the self-pity coming on. Because when you decide to let go of the nagging pity party, you're faced with today. And it's actually easier to wallow and feel crappy for yourself than it is to move on and face today with a lust for life. Because to face the day with gusto, you need to not think about what happened in the past. Not think about the dork. You need to be present—to know you're worthy and able and all right. And . . . news flash: **YOU'RE ALL RIGHT.**

ACTIVITY 13

This pity party you were throwing—what was its underlying message? What was it you thought you didn't do right? What aren't you good enough at? You know what I'm going to say: write it down. Do so under Pity Party Perceptions, on the next page.

My guess? You've written a bunch of hooey. They're untrue statements. They're perceptions of you that either you've created or someone else has, but they're not real.

So in the column next to the Pity Party Perceptions, write down a truth. Dig deep, face the facts, be present and clear minded and write down something that *sort* of contradicts your pity party perception, or maybe *completely* contradicts it, but a truth.

Pity Party Perception: I'll never love anyone like I loved him.

C'mon, you don't really believe that. It's insane.

Truth: I will love many more times in my lifetime.

This can be hard. It's often hard to write nice things about yourself, but how screwy is that? We should be able to rattle off nice things about ourselves, and yet we can't. So today it's practice time.

71

Start rattling. For every cruddy thing you wrote, for every half-truth, write a whole truth next to it. I started you off.

PITY PARTY PERCEPTIONS	TRUTH-BE-TOLD GOODNESS
I'm not good enough for him.	I'm too good for him—I'm putting real effort into bettering myself and I'll be ready when someone better for me comes along.
_____	
_____	
_____	_____
_____	_____
_____	_____
_____	_____
_____	_____
_____	_____
_____	_____
_____	_____
_____	_____

SONG OF THE DAY:
LIZ PHAIR, "NEVER SAID"

This song characterizes that sense that people are telling lies about you. Sneer along with Liz as she swears, "I never said nothing."

72

DAY FOURTEEN: WHAT IS LOVE?

Openheartedness.
That is a real word, honest.
So is trustiness.

I ask the question "What is love?" because most people don't *think* about it. They just *feel* it. But at the risk of sounding all depressing, a lot of the time we're just digging the companionship or the attention or the status that having a partner gives us. We may call it love, but it doesn't have boo one to do with love.

So let's put love on the table and discuss.

Love is pretty intense, and it can take many different forms: love for your family members, for your friends and yeah, for a cute guy. But no matter what kind of love it is, it always has *caring* as a major component.

Love is not something you can make people feel. Love is not something that can or should be used to make anybody do anything. Love is about trust and compassion and kindness.

Lust is about wanting to make out and more. Lust isn't really a component of love, although it can exist at the same time as love. If you're feeling like you want to, as Olivia Newton-John once said, get physical, but you're not feeling like you know or trust this person, well, I'm gonna go ahead and call that one lust. So to recap:

Lust is not love.

And while we're on that subject, love is not sex. Sex is not love.

Love should make you feel secure and happy and warm and fuzzy and all those other teddy bear feelings inside.

You have to know someone to deeply love them. Because you have to know who and what they value, who and what they trust and who they really are before you love them. You can't really love someone from afar. You can, however, desire to know them.

Love is not a "feeling" you get when you meet "the right person." Love is not a sensation. Love is an action.

Maintaining a loving relationship is an active endeavor, not a passive one. And although relationships can be work, love doesn't involve threats or manipulations or hurting someone intentionally.

Love is sincerity, affection, warmth, security and commitment all wrapped up into one big ball of go-go good times.

ACTIVITY 14

So go ahead and pick one or two things that love is to you. And then draw one of those goofy naked kid drawings—you know, the "Love is . . ." cartoons?

Okay, maybe not. Instead of drawing the silly cartoon, just take a few Post-its or scraps of paper and scrawl your own "Love is . . ." statements. You finish them, you fill in the blanks after those three little dots. And then stick them up around your room, on your mirror in the bathroom, under your pillow, inside your closet pinned to your favorite sweater. You don't have to keep them there forever, just long enough to really believe them, to take them inside, so that the next time you meet someone new and they're cute, you don't immediately think, "I'm in love."

HERE, I'LL GET YOU STARTED—

➤➤ Love is . . . mutual respect.

➤➤ Love is . . . genuine kindness.

➤➤ Love is . . . deep friendship.

➤➤ Love is . . . laughing your butt off.

SONG OF THE DAY:
MACY GRAY, "IT'S LOVE"

A grooving, moving song about what love is . . . and what it isn't.

DAY FIFTEEN: SPELLBOUND

He is freaky cute.
I am a smitten kitten.
But is he a jerk?

I'm gonna go out on a limb here and guess that this is how you found your ex: first you were attracted to him, thought he was cute or hot or sexy. And then, before you knew it, or him, you were entranced, you were smitten, you were "under a spell."

Maybe it didn't go quite like that, but it often does. The problem with this scenario is that you're hypnotized and you don't know what the person is actually, um, like. Is he a good guy? A nasty beast (but oh so nice to you)? It doesn't take into account what he cares about, what he's good at, what he likes to do and what he doesn't, what he believes in, how smart he is and so on and so on.

Hopefully you want more out of a relationship than just someone who looks good on your arm. You want someone you can have fun with, who makes you laugh or think or just plain feel good. And to achieve those not-so-lofty goals, you need to know something about the person first.

You also have to know what it is *you* want.

So today, that's what you're gonna think about. What do you want (besides a hottie)? What values and qualities and characteristics matter the most to you?

ACTIVITY 15

At the risk of creating a picky-picky monster, today I want you to make a list of characteristics you want in a future partner. Don't just think physical and make a list that includes "tall" and "gorgeous." Don't get me wrong, you can dream that stuff up too, if you like, but I want you to mostly cover other characteristics—intellectual things, emotional things, the person's core values.

You're gonna have to dig deep and go back a whole day to yesterday's exercise and think about how you view love. What you think love is. That will help inform today's assignment and make it more complete.

Let's start by writing down some of your own values and interests.

What do you care about? _____
Believe in? _____
Value the most in life? _____
How do you like to spend a free weekend day? _____
Name one thing that makes you laugh. _____
And something that makes you cry. _____
What is your favorite book? _____
movie?_____ band? _____
TV show?_____

Once you've covered yourself, it may be easier to clearly see what you want a boyfriend to care about too. They don't have to be the exact same things, but they should have some common ground, some correlation.

Keep it real—none of this television-inspired McDreamy stuff that isn't remotely viable, findable or doable (you're not allowed to put "is a famous [anything]" on the list). And yet don't lower your standards. This should be a genuine reflection of you and your wants.

Circle any of the following beliefs or qualities you envision your next boyfriend possessing. On the blank lines, fill in any other things I didn't think of!

BELIEVES IN: God. Saving the environment. Animal rights. Honesty.

MAKES ME: Feel comfortable. Laugh. Want to introduce him to my parents. Think about things I never did before.

ENJOYS: Hiking. Movies. Music. Comics. Plays. Reading. Watching sports on TV.

IS GOOD AT: School. Singing. Soccer. Frisbee golf. Debate.

MOST OF THE TIME IS: Outgoing. Quiet. Studious. A prankster. Easygoing. Serious. A good talker. Snarky.

LOVES HIS: Mom. Car. Pets. Friends. Nintendo Wii. Showers.

DOESN'T: Smoke. Get angry. Settle for the easy way out. Talk trash about girls.

_____

_____

_____

_____

SONG OF THE DAY:
DEATH CAB FOR CUTIE, "THE SOUND OF SETTLING"
A simple yet haunting song about not making a move, taking the easy, although considerably more unpleasant, way out and hungering for love from a distance. Listen and take to heart.

DAY SIXTEEN: YOU'RE COOL

Righteous babe you are—
Are you groovy too? Yeah,
Smart and wise and powerful.

You're more than halfway there.

If your best friend said to you, "Ugh, I'm a cow," as she dove into her second pint of Cherry Garcia, what would you say? You'd probably say something like "You are not!" and point out something great about her, give her a little pep talk, right?

So what do you do when you say to yourself, "Ugh, I'm miserable. I'm worthless"?

Do you tell yourself it ain't true?

Do you give yourself a pep talk?

Do you point out the great things you have going for yourself?

No, no and probably not.

This has got to change.

If you beat yourself up all the time, how are your beautiful strengths supposed to find their way out where they can shine?

The flip side to this coin is that to acknowledge these strengths and revel in them, you have to forgive yourself for your weaknesses. Hey, we all got 'em. The trick is to not accentuate them, but to show off your best side.

So today we make a Praise List. That way, when you're knee-deep in chocolate mint chip supreme and you want to say something horrid about yourself, you can turn to the list, look at it and give yourself a hearty pat on the back/pep talk extraordinaire because you're pretty rocking after all.

ACTIVITY 16

Thirty things. I want you to write down thirty things that are praiseworthy. They can be things you've done (or haven't done, like eaten that entire carton of ice cream) and things you have only just thought of. They can be small, like "cleaned up my room." They can be big, like "am a great big sister." They can be things like "helped my friend through a hard day" or "programmed the TiVo for Dad." They can be hobbies you enjoy. Write down anything that makes you feel happy and proud.

If you get stumped on your way to number thirty, it's time to call in some backup. Ask your best friends, your mom, your dad, even a teacher. Ask them to name a strength, something you're good at, or something you've done that made them happy recently.

Thirty things. When you're done you'll have an outline of the real and genuine person you are, even if that person feels like utter crud today. Save this list inside this book forever. Add to it from time to time. It's all you, it's yours, you own it.

❗ Turn the page for the I AM SO COOL worksheet!

SONG OF THE DAY: IMOGEN HEAP, "SHINE"

A tune about showing your best side even on your darkest days. It's as if Imogen Heap is daring herself to shine when her life is cloudy, and that is exactly what you need to do. Dare to shine through.

I AM SO COOL

1. _____
2. _____
3. _____
4. _____
5. _____
6. _____
7. _____
8. _____
9. _____
10. _____
11. _____
12. _____
13. _____
14. _____
15. _____
16. _____
17. _____
18. _____
19. _____
20. _____
21. _____
22. _____
23. _____
24. _____
25. _____
26. _____
27. _____
28. _____
29. _____
30. _____

DAY SEVENTEEN: GIVE
A LITTLE BIT

Like the Grinch, when his
Heart grew ten sizes that day,
Yours will grow big too.

There are two surefire ways to feel better. The first is to laugh. Medical science has proven that laughter has profound effects on the sick and depressed. The second thing that will ten out of ten times make you feel better? Helping someone. I've been trying to make you laugh since Day One, so let's concentrate on number two.

Maybe you've volunteered for some charity before; maybe you already know about this special feeling you get when you do something for the good of others—others you probably don't even know. But if you haven't tried it and don't know what this feeling is like, yippee-i-yay, are you in for a treat and a surprise.

Being bummed over the dork is so all about you. You, you, you. And hey, that's okay; a girl does have to take care of herself. I totally believe that. But at some point, it's important to also look completely away from you, you, you and think about the world. The bigger picture.

You are a part of a community—a bunch of communities, actually: your school, your friends, your family, your neighborhood, your city. But there is also another community you are a part of: the human race. (Cue the stirring American flag–waving music now.) And this community needs help all the time. There are folks around this world who are hurting more than you are right now, and you have the power to make them feel better. You do. It may not be direct, but you can help. For example, you might not teach children how to read, but you *can* help those children. Maybe it's by raising money for the school that will teach them to read, or maybe it's even by putting a nail into a board that holds the school up.

And as an extra added bonus, this helping others thing? Well, it makes you feel freaking great.

ACTIVITY 17

There are a zillion ways for you to volunteer. The trick is finding one that's right for you.

Start by thinking about what matters most to you:

Saving the environment? Feeding the hungry? Do you have a passion for animals? Has someone you know been afflicted with cancer? Jot down a few ideas of issues that have you concerned. And then research charities that focus on those issues. You can do this on the Web really easily.

Here are a few jumping-off points to get you started:

➤➤ Currently about fourteen million children in the United States—yes, in the U.S.—experience hunger or risk of hunger. You can volunteer by rounding up food for the largest food bank in the country, America's Second Harvest. Type in your zip at www.second harvest.org and you'll find your local chapter's phone number. Or simply enter your city and the words "food bank" into a search engine and you'll find many organizations that need assistance.

➤➤ More than five million people live at or below poverty level in the United States and more than a billion people live in poverty around the world. There are campus chapters of Habitat for Humanity at many high schools and colleges. Habitat for Humanity builds houses for needy families. And if construction isn't for you but you still want to help, they are in need of people to do all sorts of work, such as planting gardens, making welcome baskets for new homeowners, stocking the kitchens with canned goods and creating greeting cards that the organization sells to raise money. They even need babysitters! For more information about how to get involved, visit www.habitat.org and click on Get Involved.

➤➤ More than six million pets enter shelters every year. Here's a downright fun way to volunteer—become a dog walker. Most of the animal shelters need people to walk, feed and play with the animals while they wait to get adopted. Usually you commit to helping once a week or every other week. You're volunteering your time and energy and making new friends at the same time. For information on a shelter near you, go to www.Pets911.com and type in your zip code.

➤➤ Almost two hundred thousand American women are diagnosed with breast cancer each year. The Avon Foundation has donated more than four hundred million dollars worldwide for breast cancer research. They have walks in cities around the United States to raise those funds. Walking for breast cancer is a terrific way to get outside, get some exercise and raise money for an amazing cause. Can't walk that far? No sweat. You can be a crew member and sign people up, work booths or hand out water. Visit walk.avonfoundation.org for more information.

➵ Speaking of walking . . . Gather a gaggle of your best girlfriends and hit the pavement for a walkathon. Big cities usually have one a month, each for a different cause. If your city doesn't have one, create your own. Pick a charity, contact the organization and tell them you and your pals want to walk for them. Even if it's small scale, you can ask your folks and neighbors to sponsor you for five dollars a mile.

➵ Not sure what you want to do? Youth Volunteer Corps of America organizes students to do all sorts of volunteer work, from tutoring to serving meals to the homeless, from restoring park trails to eliminating graffiti. They can put you in contact with a group that's right for you. Visit www.YVCA.org to join.

➵ What about your old clothes, coats or never-to-be-worn-again prom dress? You can donate them to Goodwill, One Warm Coat (www.OneWarmCoat.org) and the Cinderella Project, respectively. If your city doesn't have one of these organizations, start your own! Contact a chapter nearby and ask them how.

➵ If you still can't find what you're looking for, you could even start your own organization or fundraising event. What can you do? Knit? Bake? Sew? Swim? Any of these things can be used to raise money for a cause you believe in. You can even sell lemonade for charity. For ideas on how to make a plan, go to www.youthnoise.com.

SONG OF THE DAY:
JACK JOHNSON, "MUDFOOTBALL"
A happy, carefree little song about the joys of being with friends and getting a little dirty. Listen while you give your time to others.

DAY EIGHTEEN: WHY, YOU LITTLE COQUETTE!

Make goo-goo eyes at—
Play footsie! Wink! Tantalize!
Flirting is quite fun!

Oh, flirting! Is there anything more delectable than being in the middle of a heady flirtation? When we are flirting we feel so alive and strong and yet oddly weak too. When we are flirting we feel in control and at the same time totally out of control, faced with the possibilities of what might happen next. Flirting is joyful. And joyful is good. It's like the real-life equivalent of whipped cream: fluffy, light, sugary—it goes straight to your head.

Flirting doesn't need to lead to anything either. It can be innocent, playful practice. It can also simply be an innocent, playful thing to do on a boring Saturday afternoon.

Flirting is part art, part science, part mystical mystery theater. But you can learn how to flirt. You can master the art part, at least.

And you're ready. The time has come. We've passed the halfway mark to recovery, and you need to practice your flirting for future fun encounters. You need to be ready, Freddy, when a new someone catches your eye.

ACTIVITY 18

Here is my primer on flirting. Read at your own risk!

STEP ONE: build your confidence. I know this is something you've been lacking of late, but it's time to turn it on. You have the ability to exude confidence. If you can grab hold of the confidence and believe in its power—even for just a few moments—you can flirt successfully. And this confidence will ultimately lead to more confidence, thereby rendering this step useless in the future because you will innately feel the confidence without me urging you to summon it from deep within.

I'll let you in on a secret: flirting is all about confidence. If you know you are worthy of this pretty parlay, it will all be so much easier, so much more natural. When you've got it, people want to know it.

STEP TWO is simple. It involves something you know how to do, even if you haven't been doing a whole lot of it these days. I'm talking about smiling. You need to try it again, out in public. You need to feel it, pull the power from inside and let it shine, shine, shine from your pearly whites. If you're having trouble because it's looking rather fake, stop. Breathe. Now think of something that truly makes you happy: a favorite toy from your childhood, an episode of your favorite show, a best-friend moment. Conjure it up in your mind and then, I promise, the smile will be oh so genuine.

Now on to the ever-important **STEP THREE**. If you've ever watched *America's Next Top Model,* maybe you've seen Miss Tyra ask the contestants to try to smile without using their mouths. She directs the girls on the show to smile with their eyes. Try it. Do it in front of the mirror. Allow yourself to crack the teeniest smile with your mouth, but mostly, feel the smile in your whole face so it has no choice but to come out in your eyes. That's the ultimate flirty smile right there, because you're saying something with those eyes. Those are no longer blank deer-in-headlights eyes; those eyes have got a story, a mysterious story, and trust me, others will want to know what it's all about.

STEP FOUR involves that slouchy back you're sporting right about now. Sit up straight. No one wants to flirt with a hunched-over ball of sludge. Stick those shoulders back, but please, stop short of thrusting your chest out for all the world to see. We want hotties to be attracted by your sparkling wit, your engaging smiling eyes and your immense capacity for caring—not your boobs.

And now you're ready for **STEP FIVE**—the conversation part. Flirting doesn't have to be rocket science or require big long conversations. Sometimes the best flirt session is short and sweet. If you've got the confidence, the smile, the smiling eyes and the stellar posture, you're already there. You're flirting. But to take it to the next step, you simply need to remember these three things:

1. **LISTEN.** No, really *listen*, hear what he's saying.

2. **REVEAL SOMETHING ABOUT YOURSELF.** No, not your address or phone number. That would be bad news—you don't even know this dude. I'm talking something vaguely silly, a dream or a favorite thing or an aspiration.

3. MAKE EYE CONTACT. You don't have to be a stalker-scary starer, but hold the eye contact a beat or two longer than you normally would before looking away. And then dramatically look away: to the left, to the floor, even to the sky, but do it with oomph.

Remember that flirting is fun and have a light-hearted good time with it—and it doesn't have to be with the best-looking guy either. Now get out there and do it! Try it out on guy friends and friends' brothers (but *not* friends' boyfriends). You're not looking for love right now. You're still exorcising the dork, so this is all in the name of practice.

> ## SONG OF THE DAY:
> ## THE SHINS, "GIRL INFORM ME"
> A song from a boy's perspective about being bewitched by a girl and her mysterious ways. Play for inspiration.

CHAPTER THREE IS OVER.

Have you stopped beating yourself up yet? Maybe. Maybe not.

But my guess is that you've moved away from self-hatred and at least a teeny tiny bit toward self-discovery. And hey, the fact that you've *moved* at all really says something about your state of mind. It may not always feel like it, but you're in the throes of self-transformation. You're more than halfway there, moving (not so effortlessly) from dumped to delicious, from cast aside to confident.

Remind yourself of this accomplishment often. The next chapter may get you down at times, but you'll be making big strides—confident, catwalk strides—over the next handful of days.

DEPRESSION

This is really what everyone's talking about when they talk about being dumped. The depression. The severe sadness that follows you around the way Lucy follows Charlie Brown around pointing out what an extreme loser he is. Well, Lucy, it's time to back away and give Chuck some space. Let him breathe.

This depression you are feeling is temporary. It's not the kind that sticks to you like rubber cement, I swear. This is the strain of depression known as dorkositus, the kind that was caught from some unsanitary attachment to a dork, and a little rest and kindness and friendship and food and imagination can make this condition evaporate into the earth's atmosphere.

This week we'll focus on the small experiences that make life powerful, enjoyable and meaningful. Breaking out of this depression isn't about one big life-changing moment, and it certainly isn't about one big life-changing new boy. In other words, don't wait for something or some*one* else to change your mood. You just need to open your eyes to the goodness and funness (yes, I made up that word— so?) that abounds around you every single solitary day. The next six days hold the secrets to small accomplishments, teeny tiny jewels of joy, nuggets of nurturing noise, aka those little droplets of perky inspiration and pure pleasure.

DAY NINETEEN: EN-DORK-PHINS!

Deem today silly
And hilariously fun—
Dress up, dance and snap!

Lethargy has set in. You can't move much, at least not with any verve or kick. That's depression for you. It grabs hold of your ankles and won't let go, causing you to squirm some but not really *get* anywhere.

But that's no good for the body, mind or soul. You need to kick-start that engine. You need more than a shove. That probably wouldn't work anyway.

What your depression needs is a little endorphin action. Running could work, but really that doesn't sound like much fun at all, now, does it? So instead, it's time to once again call upon your friends. You need their help today, and I guarantee that with an "exercise" like the one below on the table, they'll be happy to oblige.

ACTIVITY 19

It doesn't matter if you've rounded up one friend or a gaggle of girls; today you must start with a song or three. Turn it on, as loud as you're able to without the neighbors freaking out on you, and dance. Start slowly, if you must; wiggle the hips a teeny bit. But by song three I expect jumping, I expect singing along, I expect it to be like Studio 54 circa 1979 in your room with crazed sweat dripping from your forehead because your body can't help moving to the music at speeds heretofore unknown.

Once you're all revved up and you're sick with laughter because—hello?—you look silly and joyful and happy, call up your local mall photo studio, the kind that's in a Sears or Kmart or JCPenney, and make an appointment.

Yeah, a photo studio appointment. Most places will snap you for free and give you a print for less than five dollars (go online for coupons!). Make your appointment and then gather the girls.

Wigs are good. Boas. That sassy sort of thing. Or you could do yourselves up completely retro, with vivid red lips and hair flips. Flamboyant outfits are key here. And you all need to participate. Dress up, all of you, and head on down to the photo studio. Pose seriously in those getups, pose with smiles, pose every which way. Make sure you order enough pictures for each friend to have one. When you're done, place your photo prominently in your room to induce smiles later on.

🔘 If you love the idea but can't find a portrait studio, don't fret: call on a family member with a digital camera to shoot some photos of you and your friends all dolled up. If you upload them to a site like www.Snapfish.com or www.Kodakgallery.com, you can get glossy eight-by-ten photos mailed to you in a matter of days.

SONG OF THE DAY:
MORNINGWOOD, "NTH DEGREE"

Cheesy pop with an amazing dance beat. You can't *not* dance to this song, so play it loud over and over again—just be careful when you perform those rock-and-roll splits off the bed.

DAY TWENTY: WHAT TO WEAR

Wardrobe withdrawals:
Rework clothes so they are fresh.
It's like a new you!

When we're depressed, we usually look at the world with distaste. So of course everything in our closet looks old, dingy, out of style. It's our outlook, it's not the actual goods. But that's no matter; it's how you feel right now, and it's a bummer.

It's not like we can buy a whole new wardrobe every time our heart gets broken. That wouldn't be very economical. Or healthy. Still, can you bear to put on that shirt you wore so many times with the dork? Maybe. Maybe not.

The quandary is, how can we make our tired, old things look new? How can we trick ourselves into thinking everything old is fresh and peachy keen? It takes a bit of work, but it's so very doable.

And yeah, I'm not going to lie to you. Today is also about keeping your hands and your head busy. It's called distraction, and I'm a big fan.

ACTIVITY 20

This is just a good once-a-year practice to get in the habit of doing, but it might as well coincide with your depressing days. You'll kill two birdies with one hanger.

You need an honest but fair and kind friend. You know the type—she isn't going to lie and say something looks good on you if it doesn't, but she also never would make a snide remark about something that doesn't look quite right. She's forthcoming but never mean. Call her and invite her over.

Swing open your closet doors. Start on the left and try on anything you even have the slightest bit of doubt about. Your girlfriend is going to play the part of *What Not to Wear* hosts Clinton and Stacy. Only a whole lot sweeter.

The items that you two decide are out can go in a pile for the Salvation Army. The items you decide are worthy can get hung back up in the closet, much more neatly than they were before. Clothes like to be hung up all neatly, it makes them happy.

Take the questionable items, the ones that *almost*

make it or fit a little funny or have a bad memory attached to them, and put them in their own pile. When all is said and done and you've cleaned up and hauled the bad stuff away, dig into this last "almost good" pile. Ask yourself these questions:

➤➤ Can I cut this up and make something new out of it?
➤➤ Can I take it to a tailor and make it fit better for a few bucks?
➤➤ Or make it into something different altogether?
➤➤ Can I add pins, beads, jewels, iron-ons or anything else fun to make it less boring?

If the answer to any of these questions is a loud and exciting "YES!", then get busy, girl. Grab the scissors, call the tailor, collect the baubles and the needle and thread and glue and rework your clothes till they're wonderful and wacky and totally representative of the new you. Spend the whole afternoon, maybe even two, playing fashion designer and get in touch with your inner *Project Runway* self.

Here are just a few ideas of things you can do to your clothing to change it up:

➤➤ With your computer, printer and iron-on paper you get from the office supply store, you can make iron-ons touting your (fake) band and apply them to T-shirts, the back of a jacket, even a plain and boring tote bag.

➤ Hack off your jeans just below the knees, do a little basic stitching and you're ready for summer in your new capris.

➤ Sew a multitude of buttons—every size, shape and color—to the front of a T-shirt or jacket. You could even decorate the hem of a denim miniskirt this way. It's so very Marc Jacobs.

➤ Adorn a simple white tank with ruffly trim along the shoulders. Or forget the shoulders and do a gaudy yet awesome vertical stripe of ruffles right down the front.

➤ There are a million and one ways to cut a T-shirt into a whole new shape. Hit one of the many DIY Web sites, such as www.craftster.org, for instructions. In fact, with a few online tutorials you can turn all your old goods into *Project Runway*–worthy clothing like puffy-sleeved tees, sweatshirt blazers and pegged jeans.

⊗ WARNING: Before you start cutting and gluing, make sure your parents are okay with it! No need to get grounded.

DAY TWENTY-ONE:
BABY, YOU'RE A STAR

Prepare, primp, pucker!
Lights! Camera! Action! Go!
Introducing YOU!

Sometimes you just wanna be new again. Reinvent yourself. Reimagine your life as something a bit different. It's okay as long as you keep some of the characters and situations grounded in reality. And what with the zillions of reality shows on TV nowadays, you could be a hit!

Those people on *The Real World* and *Laguna Beach* and *America's Next Top Model* may be portraying themselves on TV, but they don't seem particularly real. Your show will star a star in the making, one with flaws and fabulousness, smarts and silliness. Your show will star you.

Reinvention can be a great tool, as long as you're not trying to make yourself something you're not. The idea is to bring out other, more fabulous sides of your personality, nurture them, dress 'em up and give them center stage. Besides being good for your self-esteem, it's also good for the imagination. Take the time to really think about what it is you want to project to the world. Swirl the ideas around in your head before deciding upon the new you.

But of course, you can always reinvent yourself again tomorrow.

ACTIVITY 21

Seriously, you're gonna craft your own show. Not for filming or anything. But you've watched enough television in your life that you can take some cues from the boob tube.

Now, for this make-believe show, who will be the leading lady? Duh, that's you. Can you come up with five words that describe her? "Daring?" "Brilliant?" "Hilarious?" "Creative?" **PICK THE WORDS YOU WANT OTHER PEOPLE TO DESCRIBE YOU WITH AND JOT THEM DOWN.**

_____

_____

_____

_____

_____

Next, what is this main character—this star—wearing? How does she wear her hair? And most importantly, what does she care about? **ADD THAT BELOW:**

_____

_____

_____

_____

_____

BRAINSTORMING TIME. You see those five words you just chose? Did you choose "daring" or "brilliant" or "creative?" Now it's time to work toward those goals. If you want to be smarter, hit the newspaper or spend an hour reading a book today. Want to be more creative? Pull out the paints or the pencils or the typewriter and spend some time exploring that side of you. Practice. You may not become those things overnight, but you can work toward them with time and effort.

And your supporting cast? No dork in this show! No, your castmates are your best friends, the ones who lift you up when you are down, the ones who make you laugh till Coca-Cola comes out your nose, the ones who are by your side through thick and thin. Cast members can also include cute boys seen from afar, hot brothers of friends and even the occasional foxy movie star. Hey, it's your show!

CAST: _____

_____

_____

_____

_____

Now think, where is this shooting? Is it in your hometown? Your room? Your school? Or has the location changed to somewhere exotic? And where will future episodes take place? Will they move on to a college town? Or will this show go on the road, abroad, somewhere completely new and exciting and real? Dream of places near and far.

LOCATION: _____

_____

_____

_____

HAIR AND MAKEUP TIME! Get a friend to help, one whose destiny it is to be a stylist. She can change your hairdo a zillion times till you find the ideal one for the pilot episode. She can give you smoky eyes and wash them away if you look too raccoony. She can give you baby-doll eyes with sheen and shine and curled lashes, and the poutiest lips since Angelina set her sights on Brad. Try new stuff, new looks. You don't have to be seen in them in public. It's about trial and error till you find the prettiest you.

SHOWTIME! After all the dreaming and studying and primping, it's time for your reentry into society, aka your first episode. Take it slow—it doesn't have to be a two-hour movie. Twenty minutes out and about with your friends, your new look and your new attitude will do just fine. You want this new series to last, so don't crash and burn your first night out.

Have fun with this idea. Get your girlies in on it with you and this can be a fun game to fuel your weekend nights and boring summer days for years to come. And why not? Gwyneth reinvented herself, remember? With Brad she was so Hollywood. But with Brit hubby Chris Martin she's an intellectual, organic earth mama. Sienna's a serious actress now that she's left Jude, and Kate Hudson went from young newlywed to party girl in a snap. And how many times has Madonna changed her ways?

SONG OF THE DAY:
INDIA.ARIE, "VIDEO"

An ode to self-confidence, this song sings the praises of being yourself, trying your best and being one of a kind. Play it loud and proud.

DAY TWENTY-TWO:
FENG SHWEEE

Yin-Yang, Voodoo room,
Ancient secrets. Did you know—
Turtles rock the luck.

I don't know if feng shui works. But it can't hurt, right?

A lot of people believe in it too. Not that you should jump on a bandwagon because it's popular, but at the very least, shaking up the order of your room is a good thing because it gives you a fresh perspective, a new outlook from the place where you spend many an hour: your bed.

The principle behind feng shui is that by arranging your room following various rules, you can eliminate negative energy and boost the positive stuff. The positive stuff is called chi, and this is the part of feng shui I like the best: "chi" translates to cosmic dragon's breath. How cool is that?

This dragon's breath is supposed to be able to flow through your surroundings effortlessly, without tripping on junk that's in the way. I can get behind that.

ACTIVITY 22

You're going to need a compass. You can get a cheap one at the ninety-nine-cent store, or ask a parent, friend or relative if they have one you can borrow. Stand in the center of your room and move around holding the compass. To begin, draw the shape of your room below and then mark the north, south, east and west points according to the compass. Go ahead and mark the northeast and northwest and southeast and southwest points as well. Don't draw in your furniture just yet. But do include the entry door, closet doors, windows—the things you cannot change.

Ask yourself, what direction is the door in? If it's on the north wall, your room is considered a north room. Likewise, if the door is on the south wall, your room is a south room, and so on. Each room is assigned two lucky colors. That doesn't mean you should necessarily paint your walls those colors, but they should be featured prominently, especially if you like them.

My room is a _____ room.

LUCKY COLORS:
➤➤ north room: blue and purple
➤➤ northeast room: beige and yellow
➤➤ south room: pink and orange
➤➤ southwest room: beige and yellow
➤➤ east room: green and brown
➤➤ west room: white and gray
➤➤ northwest room: gold and silver

Now make a list of all the furniture in your room. Read through the rules below, and see if you can't re-arrange your room on paper to follow some of them.

SOME RULES OF THE SHUI CHI:
➤➤ Don't put your bed in line with the door.
➤➤ Don't place the bed under a window.

➤➤ If your room is on the second floor, be careful where you put your bed in relation to what's downstairs. Don't put it over a water heater, washer or dryer or other large appliance.

➤➤ Don't put your bed under an exposed beam. If this can't be helped, then put up a canopy over your bed (you can do this with just a cool piece of fabric or a sheet or mosquito net and some rope—no need for a fancy, expensive new bedroom set.)

➤➤ Put your bed against a windowless wall.

➤➤ Do not put a TV in your room. If you must have one, cover it at night with a sheet.

➤➤ Be careful of mirrors—they should never, ever face the bed.

➤➤ Pictures of surfing and beach scenes and such are no good for the bedroom; they apparently cause bad mojo in that particular room.

➤➤ Put a crystal, if you can stand such a thing, in the southwest corner of the room. It promotes romantic feelings and energy. It can also make your life more social. Wind chimes work for this too. They should hang in the northwest corner of your room. Unless, of course, the northwest corner is where there is an air-conditioning vent. That could cause the chimes to clink and clank all night. Yikes!

➤➤ Pink and red accents are good for that loving energy, so—well, you know what to do.

➤ Never put a shelf over a desk or bed. Not just because the chi is bad, but because, um, what if it fell?

➤ Don't keep plants in the bedroom. They're full of energy, which is good in the kitchen or living room but not in the room where you need to be restful and calm.

➤ Lastly, here is a weird little factoid from the wacky world of feng shui: if you have a pet turtle, keep his little cage on the north side of the room.

Yeah, I don't know why either.

SONG OF THE DAY:
JIMMY EAT WORLD, "THE MIDDLE"

A great pep talk in the form of a pop song. You're in the middle, little girl; you got a long way to go, lots more time to be all that you want. And more.

DAY TWENTY-THREE:
YOU ARE WHAT YOU EAT

Fire, warmth, bread—ignite!
Cook now, pressing gently now.
Gooey chocolate.

Yum, donuts. They are so light and fluffy and sugary—the kind of sugar you can feel on your teeth, the kind of sugar that lingers on your tongue and in your cheeks. The dough practically melts with every bite, with barely a need to chew. They leave the most delicious residue on your fingers. What is it? Grease mixed exquisitely with more sugar! Oh, the delights of the smell and sight and taste! It's too much. Much too much.

You know that food directly affects how you feel. I mean, you may be happy as a clam eating that donut, but afterward, oh, about a half hour later, you don't feel so happy. That clam has a tummyache and is nose-diving from the sugar rush that just sent all the blood racing through her little clam body.

You eat crap, you feel like crap. You eat well, you feel better. It's a pretty straightforward mathematical equation.

But here's the kooky thing: it's not just that junk food makes us feel bad and healthy food makes us feel good. There are chemicals in certain foods that actually affect your moods. And when we're in a state of depression, it could behoove us to check into the foods that pump us up, give us energy, make us happy, rather than gorging on the foods that bring us down.

Let's run through a lesson on good-mood-inducing foods so that when you're in that sad-sack moment you don't reach for a food that's only going to make you feel worse. And don't worry, chocolate's on the good list.

ACTIVITY 23

SCIENCE LESSON #1: Carbs energize the creation of a chemical called serotonin. Serotonin makes your brain blissfully calm and happy. Ipso facto, carbs can go a long way to jump-starting your great mood. So what food combo will get you there fastest? Something low in fat and protein but high in carbs. Like a toasted whole-wheat English muffin with a spoonful of jam or a squirt of honey. Or a bowl of oatmeal with cinnamon, or a smoothie. Oh, extra bonus? You'll sleep better, tolerate pain better and manage those junk food cravings too.

SCIENCE LESSON #2: Fish is loaded with omega-3 fatty acids. I know, all those words sound so unappetizing—fatty, acids, omega, fish. But a bit of fish goes a long way, and these omega-3 jobbies not only make you happier, they make you smarter! They are linked to brain function and focus. Hate fish? You can also get some omega-3 fatty acids in this stuff called flaxseed meal. It's at every healthy food store and has little to no flavor (it's a teeny bit nutty.) It also has the happy power of omega-3s and it's actually kind of tasty sprinkled on yogurt. In a smoothie, you can't even taste it.

SCIENCE LESSON #3: And here's what you were waiting for: Chocolate. Chocolate naturally has a chemical called phenylethylamine in it. It brings us superior happy vibes. It makes us feel comforted, loved and coddled. But you can't gorge. It's got to be eaten in moderation. And here's the bummer for you Twix fans: it really shouldn't be the milky kind. Dark chocolate has way more good chemicals inside. And frankly, it's tastier. Really, I swear. Still not convinced? Try drizzling a bit of dark chocolate syrup over a bowl of cut-up fruit for a happy snack. Or have a small handful of chocolate-covered pretzels, chocolate-dipped almonds, or chocolate-covered dried apricots. Oh! The chocolate!

❽ MY FAVORITE PERKY TREAT: Take a slice of a good whole wheat bread and put a chunk of dark chocolate on it. Fold it over like a sandwich and place it in a hot pan, pressing down on the bread with a spatula so it toasts up and the chocolate melts. And then devour it. It's sort of a cross between a grilled-cheese sandwich and a chocolate croissant, two of my favorite foods!

On the next page, write down what you ate today. Do it tomorrow too. No, not to count calories or check carbs. We're conducting a slightly scientific study to see if what you eat affects your mood and energy level. Make sure to write down the times next to your snacks and meals. And then periodically come back and write down the time and your mood. Nosh on some chocolate and check back with this little mini–food diary an hour later and see if it spiked your pep or plain pooped you out.

TIME	ATE WHAT	MOOD
____	____	____
____	____	____
____	____	____
____	____	____
____	____	____
____	____	____
____	____	____
____	____	____
____	____	____
____	____	____
____	____	____
____	____	____
____	____	____

SONG OF THE DAY:
RILO KILEY, "CAPTURING MOODS"

Jenny Lewis, the girl with the golden voice, delivers a classic Rilo Kiley cryptic tune about relationships and moods. Listen while you eat that choco sandwich.

123

DAY TWENTY-FOUR:
CHI-CHI, OUI OUI

Je veux marcher comme
Une femme française et manger
Comme une femme française.

Sometimes when you're feeling down, it helps to emulate someone else, someone with confidence and je ne sais quoi. You don't have to become someone else, and you shouldn't want to, but picking up characteristics of another in an attempt to lift you out of your doldrums and give you a sheen of self-confidence, well, it's a good start.

And sometimes it's just silly fun.

Rather than picking a celebrity to emulate, because celebrities have their own mixed bag of weirdness—and really, do you want to be hounded by paparazzi 24-7?—why not pick a few characteristics.

Do you admire the supreme confidence of Brazilian women? Or the stoic serenity of Eastern European women? Personally, I'm partial to the whimsical poise that I perceive French women to have. I see them as bold yet feminine, audacious yet polished. So when I'm in a funk and feeling low, I channel my inner Frenchwoman.

No, that doesn't mean I pretend to be French, complete with a craptastic French accent. And no, I don't don a beret. I'm more interested in that inner feeling—the way I think French women carry themselves and think about themselves in relation to others. I'm looking to feel that French *femme* insolence and spirit and nerve and grace that is so Audrey Tautou in *Amélie*.

Why do French women possess this self-confidence that many American women do not? Perhaps it is their history. It's jam packed with women who played power roles yet were very feminine.

Of course, Joan of Arc was French. Joan, who was born a peasant, snuck away from her hometown and managed to get a meeting with the king about those crazy "voices" of hers that were telling her to help get the future king of France crowned. She convinced him she was right in the mind, and he produced an army for her to fight her mission. She led many successful battles and apparently was quite a good leader, before that pesky burning-at-the-stake business.

And check out the crazy story of Eleanor of Aquitaine: while still in her teens, she married Louis VII and became the Queen of France. She grew up to be headstrong and passionate, and after fifteen years of marriage, she left Louis. Within a matter of weeks she married the King of England's grandson, who was more than ten years younger than she was. Two years later, he's King Henry II and she's the Queen of freaking England. She loved poetry and music so much that they became important to her subjects as well, making her a major source of France's long love of literature. While kings were "in charge" of France for hundreds of years, history tells a different story, revealing the wives and mistresses of the kings to have been very powerful, often pulling the strings.

ACTIVITY 24

To channel your inner Frenchwoman (or Brazilian or Serbian or African woman), start by looking up a famous woman from history online. Read a short essay on her and glean from it all her righteous, self-confident power.

As you leave your house today, imagine her in your head. Is she walking taller than you? Well, then straighten that back, lift your chin just a bit higher. Does she clomp or glide when she walks in your mind's eye? Well, then move with an elegant deliberation.

Put just a little more thought into your walk. Place one foot directly in front of the other, as if you're walking a balance beam; it causes your hips to sway naturally, with a hint of exaggeration. Don't lunge with your head forward as we so often do, on a mission with a place to be. Slow down; savor the walk.

Now, do you think your inner woman's eyes flared with a fire inside? Probably so. You don't make history without fire in your eyes. So find your fire: you're feeling self-confident, you're feeling unflappable, you're feeling chic, so let that fire roar up inside you. It will find your eyes.

If you're emulating a French femme fatale, listen to sixties French music like Chantal Goya and Françoise Hardy, Serge Gainsbourg and Claudine Longet. Watch a French film such as *Breathless* (the original from 1960 with Jean Seberg) or *The Umbrellas of Cherbourg* (the movie dialogue is entirely sung) or the mad drama of *Camille Claudel*, a biopic of the French sculptor. Pick up a croissant, some cheese, a few pieces of fruit and chunks of chocolate and eat like a Parisian.

If you're not looking to channel your Frenchwoman but your role model from another part of the world, explore the art and culture and food of that country today. Soak it up, breathe it in and soon you'll be walking and talking with just a hair more confidence than before.

CHAPTER FOUR IS OVER.

And you've probably figured out by now that the last
six days weren't so much about depression but about
making you happy. Or rather, getting you to recog-
nize the things about your life that already make you
happy. Getting you to open your eyes, open your
heart and soak them in.

It's amazing how wondrous our own superhero
powers are. We have the lightning-fast ability to
change our own mood, move on from the past and
create our own futures. If only we had a magic truth-
telling lasso, we'd be as powerful as Wonder Woman.

But you know, truth-telling, in some instances
(like when the truth hurts), isn't all it's cracked up to
be. So revel in your remarkable and finely tuned
powers right now, because you are almost all done.

ACCEPTANCE

Ah, we're in the homestretch.

Here's what I have found over the years: during my gray days—and you're in your gray days; the black days have now passed—little signs of new growth appear. Just like a sprout taking hold in the soil. These signs I'm talking about, they're the flashes of inspiration and the small "aha's!", the really cool dreams and the slow-burning passion rising up from your gut, the teeny voice you hear in your ear egging you on to do powerful and amazing things, things that have absolutely nothing to do with the dork.

It's now time to clear the path and make way for

these new seeds to take hold so the sprout can grow up big and strong into some killer tree that will eventually give shade and comfort to you and those around you.

Whoa, I got super-new agey there for a second. But you know what I mean.

It's time in this new stage of acceptance to keep our eyes wide open and take some cues from our restless new selves. We need to make time for our new interests and our new dreams.

To be happier day to day, we need to cultivate these dreams. Because buying new shoes and getting a cooler phone is only going to bring you pleasure for a fleeting moment. But becoming the person you want to be, exploring the things you're curious about and becoming physically and emotionally stronger, well, those things bring you happiness over and over and for years to come. It's normal to feel lousy sometimes, it really is. We shouldn't be happy all the time. If we were, then it wouldn't feel the same. With no downs, the ups would just feel flat. But that doesn't mean we should stop striving to make the most of life. And that's what this chapter, the final chapter to getting over that dork, is all about.

DAY TWENTY-FIVE:

DESTINY'S CHILD

Make a move, baby,
Or nothing will happen.
Well, nothing you want.

Okay, so we talked all about dreams. Dreams rock. They inspire and give us a glimpse of what we want from life. But of course, your destiny isn't really in your dreams. It's in your actions.

Some things occur accidentally, by happenstance. You can sit around and wait for things to start happening around you. I call that the "sofa spud" approach to life. But really, that seems sort of unproductive, doesn't it? (Not to mention boring.)

Things can also happen because you make them happen—you take action. You just need to draw up a little plan. A map of sorts.

Which leads us back to those dreams . . .

Care to dream a little dream with me? Fill in the blanks below.

What are you thinking about even when you should be doing something else (besides the dork)? _____

_____

Is there something you feel inspired to share with people? An idea? A song? A painting or a drawing? A thought? A story? _____

_____

Is there something you want to do or try so badly it hurts? _____

_____

If you were allowed to make one powerful change in this world, large or small, what would it be? _____

_____

Name five things you care about—family can be one, but go beyond your small world, go further than just what's in front of you and think about life beyond your four walls and your friends.

1. _____
2. _____
3. _____
4. _____
5. _____

What personal challenges have you overcome? (One I can think of is you got over the dork. Put that down, but come up with at least one other.) _____

_____

If you could explore three types of jobs for your future, what would they be?

1. _____
2. _____
3. _____

Spend the day going back to these questions and adding more answers. Tomorrow, we'll address what they mean and how to turn them into something more than just a wish or a thought.

SONG OF THE DAY:
JASON MRAZ, "SONG FOR A FRIEND"
This friend apparently had a profound effect on Mraz, who sings about his pal's uplifting words about loving yourself and finding your inner strengths. It's a quiet song about a really loud concept, so play it accordingly.

DAY TWENTY-SIX: JUST DO IT

Things you will do now,
Passion-promises you make—
Don't let yourself down.

Yesterday you wrote down answers to my lovely questions. Read over the answers. Is there a pattern? Is there one or are there two or even three things that keep coming up, like painting or writing or fashion or helping others? Look for that nugget that is buried in more than one of your answers. That nugget is what we're gonna concentrate on today.

That nugget—that's your passion.

"Passion" is a funny word. All too often we think of it as a fiery feeling we get for someone else. Like, "I love him so much, I have soooo much passion for him." Yeah, okay, whatever. It's not grammatically incorrect or anything. But passion is so much more than what you feel for some guy.

Passion is what delights you, inspires you, calls you to action. Passion ignites your imagination and fuels your desires. And your passion goes a long way to making you, well, you.

Sometimes we get so busy, what with school and extracurricular stuff and friends and that dork, that we miss out on experiencing the pulse-pounding excitement we can get when we pursue our passion. But in those moments when we feel the passion, we are moved. We are struck. We feel deeply and soulfully. Besides making us happy, those moments make us better people and much more inclined to get out there and, in the immortal words of the advertisers who made a buttload of money for Nike, Just Do It.

ACTIVITY 26

Now it's time for the action: that passion you discovered in your answers—how can you pursue it? This is the question of the day.

On the next page, go ahead and list five things you can do to explore that passion. Five things that will lead you closer to the realization of your dream. I want them to be five *actions*. Not just more thoughts, but things you can do right now.

And it's okay if you don't know much about this

passion yet. It's okay for it to be something you know nothing about. It's okay to make mistakes or do something badly. It's okay if you can't decide on one passion. If that's the case, pick two, and make two lists. The whole thing is a process. So now, on to those five actions.

Think about things like—
➤➤ Talking with someone who has a similar passion.
➤➤ Visiting the library and researching this passion.
➤➤ Spending an afternoon with the passion in some way.
➤➤ Meeting new people who share this passion.
➤➤ Signing up for a class or club that is about this passion.
➤➤ Creating your own club to focus on your passion.
➤➤ Reading a great book on your passion.
➤➤ Volunteering for an organization that is based on your passion.
➤➤ Setting aside time to practice your passion.
➤➤ Creating a blog dedicated to your passion.

These are all actions.

MY PASSION is _____

_____

_____

_____

_____

_____

My action plan:

_____

_____

_____

_____

_____

This list of five things is your Action Plan. Decorate the borders and make it all pretty. And then get started. Pick one thing from the list that you can do *today*.

And Just Do It.

DAY TWENTY-SEVEN:
FAMILY MATTERS

Annoying? Oh yes,
But lovely and generous.
You are stuck with them.

Family is a funny thing. I mean, sometimes they annoy the crap out of you, but other times, their comfort is better than anything else. It's that way, I think, in your genes too. Some of the things you've inherited from your ancestors are wonderful and joyous, and others, not so much.

Today I want you to think about all the rad stuff you inherited from your folks and their folks and so on. Maybe none of those great things comes to mind. That means it's time to hit the paper and pen and do a little historical digging.

Why should you care? Because your grandfather

or great-aunt may have been or done something outstanding. Something that rings true with you, something you feel connected to, something you could have done yourself, maybe, if things were different, if times were different. Maybe even something you could still do in the future (you do have many years ahead of you, just waiting to be filled up with accomplishments and experiences). This exercise may just reveal little bits of who you are that you didn't even notice were there. All in all, we're looking for a little inspiration in the back pages of your very own herstory.

Maybe you won't find anything. But maybe you will.

And if you don't, feel free to make it up. No, I'm not kidding. Create a backstory that will propel you to action, propel you toward great things.

ACTIVITY 27

Copy the chart on the next page onto a large piece of paper. Take a peek at the directions. You can begin by just filling in the name of the person who belongs in that box, then go back and add the rest of the information:

Each box should have the number in it and then the following fill-in-the-blanks:

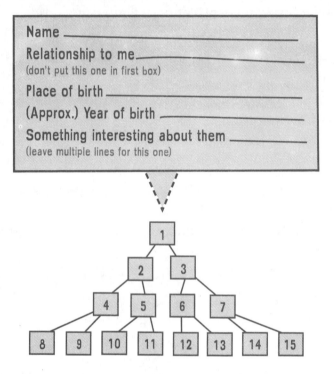

Name _____

Relationship to me_____
(don't put this one in first box)

Place of birth _____

(Approx.) Year of birth _____

Something interesting about them _____
(leave multiple lines for this one)

➤➤ Start with yourself. Your name goes in box 1.

➤➤ Your dad goes in box 2 and your mom in box 3.

➤➤ Your dad's dad goes in box 4 and your dad's mom goes in box 5.

➤➤ Fill in your mom's dad's name in box 6 and your mom's mom's name in box 7.

➤➤ Can you keep going? Boxes 8 and 9 should have the dad and mom of box 4 (your paternal grandpa), respectively.

➤ Boxes 10 and 11 should have the dad and mom of box 5 (your paternal grandma), respectively.
➤ Boxes 12 and 13 should have the dad and mom of box 6 (your maternal grandpa), respectively.
➤ Boxes 14 and 15 should have the dad and mom of box 7 (your maternal grandma), respectively.
➤ Feel free to add side boxes for siblings of these various relatives.

Now go back and fill in any information in the boxes where you know the answer. Fill in that relative's name, place of birth and year of birth (approximate if necessary). If you get stumped, go ask other family members. Try a grandma or a grandpa; they love this junk. And now ask more questions to reveal more tales. That's how you get the good stuff—you ask.

But what to ask? How about some of these terrific historical conversation starters:

➤ Who were you named after?
➤ Does your name have any special meaning?
➤ Where did you grow up?
➤ What was it like?
➤ How was it different from today?
➤ Did you have any special traditions with your family?
➤ What were your hobbies?

➤ What were your biggest challenges?

➤ Where are the rest of our relatives—in other parts of the country? The world?

And even though your parents aren't that old, they still could give you some surprising answers to these sorts of questions, because the world is changing fast. Things are different from when they were young. So ask questions. Ask anyone in your family you can get your hands on. Call them up. E-mail them. But ask.

SONG OF THE DAY:
THE DONNAS, "40 BOYS IN 40 NIGHTS"
One of the most hilarious songs ever recorded finds this band of girls leaving a trail of boy dust in their wake as they travel from town to town, breaking hearts. Gather your friends and sing along loudly, imagining yourselves as boisterous, butt-kicking Donnas.

DAY TWENTY-EIGHT:
YOU'VE COME A LONG WAY, BABY

Accomplishments rock!
You were dumped, so what of it?
Life is moving on.

Look back on this book, the exercises you've completed and the things you've learned about yourself as you made your way from the beginning to the (almost) end. Jot down a few notes about those precious things you've learned.

_____

_____

_____

_____

_____

Had you not been dumped, you would not have learned those things. Well, at least not so soon.

145

Now make a quick list of the things that really sucked about the dork. Jot 'em down. Don't spend a whole lot of time thinking about it, just list the things that have truly stuck with you these twenty-eight days.

_____

_____

_____

_____

Look at that list.

Those are the things to avoid in the next boyfriend.

If you spot those traits in another guy, no matter how cute he is, walk away. Those are things you've learned do not sit well with you. They are not compatible with you. And even if he is très foxy, it doesn't matter. Those things will come back to haunt you in the end.

ACTIVITY 28

Those things you just jotted down—the list of things you've learned about yourself and the qualities you don't want in another boy—let's *really* write 'em down. It's our last letter of the book.

Now proceed to tell the dork all the wonderful things you learned from the dumping. How in the end, it's turned out to be a really and truly positive experience because you are a better person for it.

Begin like this:

Dear Dork,

Breaking up with you ended up being a good thing. See, I've learned about the qualities I need from my next boyfriend, things like [fill in positive qualities you want from your next guy]

_____

_____

_____

and I've also learned what I don't want: [fill in negative qualities the Dork had that you don't want in your next guy] _____

_____

_____ .

You've actually helped me become more discerning about guys and now my future relationships will be a zillion times better because I know who I am and what I want.

I've really made progress since we split. I'm trying new things such as _____

_____

_____ .

I'm taking chances I would not have dreamed of before and I've even found my passion. I truly enjoy [fill in passion here and at least one action] _____

_____

_____ .

So thank you.

I wish you all the best, [No need for X's and O's here.]

_____
[Signature]

147

❷ And now—of course—**DON'T** send it.

I know it can be tempting, but remember, we never, ever send break-up letters of any kind. (E-mails count!) They can come back to haunt us in the end, and they usually do. They can make their way into the wrong person's hands, and that's opening up a whole other can of worms.

This letter is a proclamation of the new you and a document that declares to all what you have learned from the dork and his poor, poor handling of you and your relationship. You've officially taken back your sanity, your happiness, your passion, your dreams and your life.

Congratulations, truly.

If you find that you're having a moment sometime in the future when you doubt yourself and all that you've learned, go ahead and open this book to this page, to this wonderful piece of prose, and read it, devour it, feel it, become it all over again.

SONG OF THE DAY:
JEFF BUCKLEY, "LAST GOODBYE"

In a letter inside a song, this captivating (and deliciously gorgeous) singer tells his mate that he's better for the relationship even though it's over. Your sentiments exactly. Listen while you craft your own letter.

DAY TWENTY-NINE: IT'S A BIG, BIG WORLD OUT THERE

More than six billion,
Five hundred and twenty-three
Million people here

It's so easy to get caught up in what's in front of you: your house, your family, your circle of friends, your neighborhood, your school.

But of course, life goes on outside that small sphere that is your life. There is a huge world out there full of interesting, exciting and wondrous people you've never met. (And as an added bonus, a good chunk of them are boys.) There are places that are unlike anything you've ever seen before. There are countries and cities and mountains and beaches and farms and towns that are wildly different from everything you already know.

149

Aren't you the least bit curious?

People who study abroad and travel and explore generally have bigger ideas about the world. They feel more invested in making it a better place. They have a better understanding of other cultures, more generosity for people who are unlike them and a more peaceful approach to the unknown. People who travel can see firsthand what it's like to live with less, or more; to live under wildly different circumstances; to live halfway around the world.

Even if you cannot get away physically today, you can get away mentally and set the plan in motion for the future, when you can grow wings and fly.

ACTIVITY 29

This is an ongoing exercise. Do it today, yes, but whenever you've got a little time, do it again, and again, and again.

Got a globe? Spin it with your eyes closed and put your finger down. Open your eyes. Where did it land? You can do the same thing with an atlas or a map of the world. If you don't have such a thing, hit the library or pick one up—a girl should always have a good map.

Now that you have your "place of the day," investigate it. Google it or look it up in the library. Find out who lives there, what they do and eat, what kind of music they listen to. What are the politics like? Is it a dangerous place? A tight-knit community? What is the terrain like? What can a tourist do there? Is it anything like where you live? Or completely and utterly different? What language do the people speak? What is the place most known for? Read about it, look at pictures and allow yourself some quiet time to dream about being there, visiting and getting to know the people and the place.

Another way to accomplish this goal of traveling without actually traveling is to pick up travel magazines. You know where I find them? No, not the magazine stand for four dollars a pop. There are always stacks of travel mags at local thrift stores for like a quarter apiece. And the library often has a small box of books and magazines that people have donated for sale, and I've found it's loaded with travel titles. Often they're a dime apiece, or even free. It doesn't matter if they're a few years old; the articles still brim with the sounds and sights of the exotic locales. When you come across places you think sound amazing or peculiar or just plain interesting, rip out the articles and put them in a special box or folder. Mark it "The Places I Will Go." And refer back to it whenever you want to hit the road. The future holds many opportunities for you; you're that much more prepared to take them now.

PLACES I WILL GO

I want to travel to_____ and see _____
_____ . While I'm there I will taste_____ .

I want to travel to _____ and take photographs of
_____ . While I'm there I will try my hand
at speaking _____ .

I want to travel to _____ and go on _____ .
While I'm there I will pick up souvenirs like _____
_____ .

I want to travel to _____ and stay at _____ .
While I'm there I will visit _____ .

Other places I will go: _____
_____
_____
_____ .

DAY THIRTY: THE BEGINNING

You're ready, girl.
Live life with stars in your eyes.
Love every moment.

Congratulations—you have completed the Getting Over the DORK You <u>Used</u> to Call Your Boyfriend challenge. To say I'm proud of you is an understatement. I think you rock. And roll.

No "Activity" today, but I do want you to do something: I want you to reward yourself. You've gone through a lot these last thirty days, and in the process you've worked hard and accomplished much. You deserve a prize.

There is a small hitch. And hey, you can do what you want—if you need a new pair of shoes and you've got the cash, then go for it. But here's what I'd like to see you do with that there reward. I'd like to see you go have fun with your friends, as opposed to buying something.

I'd like to see you go do something silly and ridiculous and flirtatiously fun with your friends. Like, throw a little congratulatory party with lots of meaningless pop songs and yummy snacks.

Or drive around to every Baskin-Robbins and Ben & Jerry's in town and request samples galore, never ever actually buying any ice cream.

Or mark this day by having you and your friends communicate only through song lyrics! That's right, sing your way through the day.

Or maybe you and your friends can hold an all-girl poker tournament at your house, and instead of money, you play with gummy bears. Don't forget to dress up in ridiculous outfits; everything is better when you're wearing ridiculous outfits.

Or maybe you could grab the TV and the DVD player and a long, oh-so-long extension cord and you can have a movie-fest in your backyard. Pop some corn, kick back on the outdoor chaise lounges and watch a Molly Ringwald marathon or a Drew Barrymore marathon or another cool and quirky actress chick marathon.

Or you could gather the girlies together to create a magazine about something or someone you all love. And you can do it in one crazy, fun-filled night. Assign stories and start clipping photos out of other magazines and altering them with markers and glitter. Get everything laid out and glue it down with glue sticks and then take it to a photocopier place (they're usually open twenty-four hours anyway) and get to work making copies. Distribute your new zine all over town. Or just keep it for yourselves.

Or you and your friends could all plant little flower gardens in your bike baskets and then go on a parade all around the neighborhood and all around town. Yes, it's absurd, and yes, it's silly, but that's the point.

Because by rewarding yourself with a fun activity, you're rewarding yourself with a rousing good memory, a wonderfully delicious memory. And like I've said before, the good feeling you get from that memory is something you can return to again and again and again. You can't say the same about those shoes once they go out of style.

Seriously, congratulations!
Here's to fewer dorks in our lives—

With much love and respect,

Clea

P.S. Your final Song of the Day is
GLORIA GAYNOR'S ANTHEM "I WILL SURVIVE."
You know what to do. XO

Certificate of Vast Achievement

On this _____ Day of _____,
              [numeral]   [month & year]

_____
   [your name]

is hereby recognized for

Righteous Excellence, Spirited Self-Possession, and
Discharge of the Dork.

This Certifies that _____ is officially Over the Dork.
                         [your name]

Awarded by Clea Hantman *Clea Hantma*

with the utmost praise and respect.

GIRLS WHO HAVE DUMPED
WITH APLOMB

➤➤ ➤➤ ➤➤ ➤➤

➤➤ Cartimandua, Queen of the Brigantes

➤➤ Queen Elizabeth I

➤➤ Gwyneth Paltrow (dumped Ben Affleck and Brad Pitt—future dumpers themselves)

➤➤ Julia Roberts (dumped multiple men, even one at the altar)

➤➤ Sadie Frost (dumped the very hot but very naughty Jude Law)

➤➤ Jessica Simpson (dumped that lump of a husband)

➤➤ Renée Zellweger (dumped her country hubby of four months)

➤➤ Serena Williams (dumped boyfriend Brent Ratner after he partied for a week straight with P. Diddy)

➤➤ Naomi Watts (dumped Heath Ledger because he was too immature)

➤➤ Cameron Diaz (dumped Matt Dillon)

➤➤ Dita Von Teese (dumped creepy Marilyn Manson when she learned of his even creepier wandering eye)

➤➤ Reese Witherspoon (dumped her cheating hubby Ryan Phillippe)

➤➤ Mandy Moore (dumped Zach Braff)

GIRLS WHO HAVE BEEN MORE FAMOUSLY DUMPED THAN YOU

(And Lived to Tell!)

- **Jennifer Aniston** (dumped by Brad Pitt)
- **Nicole Kidman** (dumped by Tom Cruise)
- **Madonna** (dumped by Sean Penn)
- **Minnie Driver** (Matt Damon dumped her on *Oprah*)
- **Isabelle Adjani** (dumped—repeatedly by fax—by Daniel Day-Lewis)
- **Renée Zellweger** (dumped by Jack White)
- **Kate Moss** (dumped by Johnny Depp)
- **Mandy Moore** (dumped by Elijah Wood and Andy Roddick)
- **Lindsay Lohan** (dumped by everyone)
- **Jennifer Lopez** (dumped by Ben Affleck)
- **Tara Reid** (dumped by Carson Daly)
- **Britney Spears** (dumped by Justin)
- **Cameron Diaz** (dumped by Justin too!)
- **Mary-Louise Parker** (dumped when she was seven months pregnant by her boyfriend, actor Billy Crudup, who immediately took up with the much younger Claire Danes—eww!)

MOVIES ABOUT BEING DUMPED

➤➤ ➤➤ ➤➤ ➤➤

➤➤ *Cruel Intentions*
➤➤ *Can't Hardly Wait*
➤➤ *Elizabethtown*
➤➤ *Get Over It*
➤➤ *High Fidelity*
➤➤ *In Good Company*
➤➤ *Mallrats*
➤➤ *Singles*
➤➤ *Reality Bites*
➤➤ *Next Stop Wonderland*
➤➤ *Sandra Gets Dumped*
➤➤ *She's All That*
➤➤ *The Wedding Singer*
➤➤ *Bridget Jones's Diary*
➤➤ *Grease*
➤➤ *Better Off Dead*
➤➤ *Mystic Pizza*
➤➤ *Fatal Attraction* (!)
➤➤ *40 Days and 40 Nights*

MORE BREAKUP SONGS

➤➤ ➤➤ ➤➤ ➤➤

➤➤ The Cure, "Pictures of You"

➤➤ Psychedelic Furs, "The Ghost in You"

➤➤ Oasis, "Don't Go Away"

➤➤ Beck, "Guess I'm Doing Fine"

➤➤ Death Cab for Cutie, "A Lack of Color"

➤➤ They Might Be Giants, "Lucky Ball and Chain"

➤➤ Lauryn Hill, "Ex-Factor"

➤➤ Garbage, "Cup of Coffee"

➤➤ Green Day, "Good Riddance (Time of Your Life)"

➤➤ The J. Geils Band, "Love Stinks"

➤➤ Ani DiFranco, "Sorry I Am"

➤➤ Cake, "Never There"

➤➤ Moby, "At Least We Tried"

➤➤ The Cranberries, "Linger"

➤➤ U2, "With or Without You"

➤➤ Rilo Kiley, "Does He Love You?"

➤➤ Feist, "Inside and Out"

➤➤ Blur, "No Distance Left to Run"

➤➤ M. Ward, "Oh, Take Me Back"

➤➤ Sondre Lerche, "On and Off Again"

➤➤ Coldplay, "Trouble"

➤➤ Ben Lee, "No Room to Bleed"

➤➤ Trespassers William, "Alone"

➤➤ Donovan Woods, "I Ain't Saying She's Better Than You"

BOOKS ABOUT THE UPS, DOWNS AND IN-BETWEENS OF RELATIONSHIPS

➤➤ ➤➤ ➤➤ ➤➤

➤➤ *Bridget Jones's Diary*, by Helen Fielding
➤➤ *The Sisterhood of the Traveling Pants*, by Ann Brashares
➤➤ *The Boyfriend List*, by E. Lockhart
➤➤ *Angus, Thongs and Full-Frontal Snogging*, by Louise Rennison
➤➤ *Getting the Girl*, by Markus Zusak
➤➤ *Burger Wuss*, by M. T. Anderson
➤➤ *One Hot Second*, edited by Cathy Young
➤➤ *Nick and Norah's Infinite Playlist*, by Rachel Cohn and David Levithan
➤➤ *Shattering Glass*, by Gail Giles
➤➤ *Slumming*, by Kristen D. Randle
➤➤ *Tantalize*, by Cynthia Leitich Smith
➤➤ *Thou Shalt Not Dump the Skater Dude and Other Commandments I Have Broken*, by Rosemary Graham
➤➤ *Unexpected Development*, by Marlene Perez
➤➤ *Girl: A Novel*, by Blake Nelson
➤➤ *Vegan Virgin Valentine*, by Carolyn Mackler
➤➤ *Top Ten Uses for an Unworn Prom Dress*, by Tina Ferraro

CLEA HANTMAN has been dumped—many, many times. But she's learned from her mistakes. She's the author of ten books for young women and has worked in advertising for the likes of Target, Wet Seal, Urban Decay, and Hello Kitty. Each and every week she delivers advice to the girls at Girlsense.com in her spunky and straightforward Super Clea column. Clea lives in San Diego with her husband and daughter. You can visit her at her blog, www.GettingOverTheDork.com.